The Rest of
THE BIBLE

*A Guide to the Old Testament
of the Early Church*

Prayer of Manasseh

Psalm 151

1, 2, and

Wisdom of Solomon

Wisdom of Sirach

Baruch

The Epistle of Jeremiah

Susanna

Bel and the Dragon

The Song of the Three Holy Youths

THERON MATHIS

CONCILIAR
PRESS
Chesterton, Indiana

THE REST OF THE BIBLE
A Guide to the Old Testament of the Early Church

Copyright © 2011 by Theron Mathis

Published by
    Conciliar Press
    A division of Conciliar Media Ministries
    PO Box 748
    Chesterton, IN 46304

All Old Testament quotations, unless otherwise identified, are from the Orthodox Study Bible, © 2008 by St. Athanasius Academy of Orthodox Theology (published by Thomas Nelson, Inc., Nashville, Tennessee) and are used by permission. New Testament quotations are from the New King James Version of the Bible, © 1982 by Thomas Nelson, Inc., and are used by permission.

Photo of author (on back cover), by Vest Advertising.

ISBN 10: 1-936270-15-3
ISBN 13: 978-1-936270-15-6

To my wife, Beth

Nothing would happen without you.

(1 Ezra 4:13–17)

Contents

 # *The Readables*

" . . . appointed by the Fathers to be
read by those who newly join us,
and who wish for instruction in the
word of godliness . . . "
—*St. Athanasius, Festal Letter 39* [1]

A beautiful widow risks her life to defend her people while men cower in fear. A reprobate king repents and miraculously turns back toward God. A Jewish exile plays a game of riddles in a Persian king's court. A young man faces down a demon in order to marry a woman seven times widowed. Young men and widows become martyrs in the face of idolatry. Wisdom is detailed and exalted. Christ is revealed.

These and many other stories make up this collection of books we are about to explore—authentic books of the Bible you've probably never read. These books have gone by many names—Protestants call them the Apocrypha, Roman Catholics call them the Deutero-canonicals. But St. Athanasius, a fourth-century Church Father who was instrumental in establishing the Christian canon of Scripture, referred to them as the *Anagignoskomena*, or the Readables.

WHAT ARE THE READABLES?

The Readables are those books and sections of books that are included in the Septuagint—the Greek translation of the Hebrew Scriptures made about 200 years before Christ—but were subsequently omitted from the Hebrew canon approved by Jewish scholars in the

---

1   St. Athanasius, Festal Letter 39. Nicene and Post-Nicene Fathers Series 2, Volume 4, Philip Schaff (ed.), p. 552

tenth century AD (the Masoretic Text). This Hebrew canon was then adopted by the Reformers instead of the Septuagint when they created their translations of the Bible.

The Reformers used the term *Apocrypha* for the Greek books to suggest their unworthiness as Scripture. The word *apocrypha* means "hidden," and thus these books came to be seen as scandalous and harmful to read. As a result, when printed, they were often included as an appendix, and eventually they were simply left out.

Roman Catholics, though they include most of the Greek books in their Bibles, often place them in a separate section and refer to them as the Deuterocanonicals, suggesting they are secondary in importance to the real canon. This is problematic because it diminishes the significance of these books. The Catholic use of this term is a concession to the Reformers; it was officially bestowed at the Counter-Reformation Council of Trent.

The Fathers of the Church, while realizing these books could only be found in Greek, accepted them because they were part of the Septuagint, which had been the Church's Old Testament since the first century. (Some of these books have lately been discovered in Hebrew manuscripts as well.) The Readables were accepted universally as fully canonical Scripture for the first fifteen hundred years of the Christian Church.

The Readables are not placed in a separate section in the Septuagint, but are interspersed throughout the Old Testament. St. Athanasius and many other Church Fathers included these books as part of the catechism for those preparing for baptism, due to the clear moral teaching they convey and the virtuous life they exemplify.

Other Orthodox over the years have called this collection "the Greek books" or "the ecclesiastical books." To follow St. Athanasius, throughout this text we will refer to them as the Readables. The following books and portions of books comprise the Readables:

The Prayer of Manasseh (found in 2 Chronicles)
Psalm 151
1 Ezra (2 Ezra is the same as the Protestant Ezra)

Tobit

Judith

Additions to Esther

1, 2, and 3 Maccabees

The Wisdom of Solomon

The Wisdom of Jesus, Son of Sirach (Ecclesiaticus)

Baruch

The Epistle of Jeremiah

Portions of Daniel (Susanna, Bel and the Dragon, The
  Song of the Three Holy Youths)

WHEN WERE THE READABLES WRITTEN?

To answer this question, a short overview of biblical history is helpful.

The first five books of the Old Testament, called the Pentateuch, are traditionally ascribed to Moses. These books cover a lot of history—from Creation to Abraham (2000 BC) and the Exodus (1400 BC). After the Pentateuch, the historical books cover the history of Israel from the entry into the Promised Land up to the beginning of the Davidic monarchy: another 400 years (1000 BC makes for an easy estimated date to remember for King David and Solomon). After Solomon, the kingdom of Israel was divided into Northern Israel and Southern Judah. Northern Israel, due to its pagan nature and rejection of the God of Israel, was eventually captured and destroyed by the Assyrians in about 700 BC. The destruction of Israel became a refrain for many of the prophets of Judah as they warned their people of a similar fate to come.

Southern Judah held out until the Babylonians invaded and exiled the population to Babylon for seventy years, beginning in about 600 BC. The exiles eventually returned under the Persian Empire to rebuild Jerusalem and their society. Shortly after the return, Alexander the Great appeared on the scene of world history and subdued Persia. He established the Greek Empire, which lasted until the next major power, Rome, conquered the civilized world. Not many decades after the rise of Rome, the events of the New Testament began.

The composition dates of the Readables are scattered across the end of the Davidic monarchy, the Babylonian captivity, the return under Persia, and the dominance of the Greek empires. The majority of the books fall during the Persian and Greek periods. They often contain a Jewish response to the paganism of Greece and the philosophical influence of Greek ideas.

WHY READ THE READABLES?

Why should we bother studying and learning about these books? First and foremost, the Orthodox Church has read and cherished them from early times because they provide us with an encounter with Christ. Also, as seen above, St. Athanasius and many other early Christians saw these books as important enough to be required reading for catechumens and new believers, due to their important moral content.

Many Christians in the English-speaking world have had a lack of access to these books. Indeed, anyone with a Protestant background may never have read them. As a result, the books may seem mysterious or forbidden. But Christ is found in these pages. The Church uses them in her services. Heroes and martyrs are present here. And on top of all that, they are full of stories that are exciting and fun to read—indeed, *readable*.

The purpose of this book is to give Christians an introduction to these unique books. It is in no way an academic or thorough treatment of the books or all the issues surrounding them. My desire is to give enough information to prod you into prayerful reading, meditation, and perhaps study of these wonderful books.

For each book, we will outline its basic structure and summarize its major highlights. Then we will choose a passage or two for focus and meditation. We will also discuss how each book is read within the Orthodox Church. Orthodox Christianity teaches that Scripture is only understood rightly within the context of the Church, through the lens of the Person of Christ and the events of His Passion. So for each book, we will look at comments from the Fathers and examine when and where these books are used in the Church's liturgy.

All of the Readables are included in their entirety in the *Orthodox Study Bible*, the Old Testament of which was translated directly from the Septuagint. A glance at the Table of Contents will show you where to find them. Pick up an OSB and read along!

 # The Prayer of Manasseh & Psalm 151

BACKGROUND

The first two sections we will cover are really small passages rather than total books. The first, found at the end of the Book of 2 Chronicles, is the prayer of the repentant Manasseh, King of Judah. The second is Psalm 151, a short autobiographical psalm that recounts events in the life of David. This psalm, like the Prayer of Manasseh, is not included in the Hebrew manuscripts but is found at the end of the Septuagint version of the Psalter.

First, let's examine the Prayer of Manasseh. Manasseh was king in the waning days of the kings of Judah. He was the son of the godly king of Judah, Hezekiah, yet he was far from sharing the righteousness of his father.

Hezekiah's story can be found in the books of Kings, Chronicles, and Isaiah. Miraculous events characterized his life. The Assyrian horde threatened to annihilate Jerusalem just as it had the Northern Kingdom, but Hezekiah stood in prayer before God, and the armies of heaven struck the invaders and drove them back. At one time, Hezekiah was near death, but due to his prayer God spared his life for several more years. When he did die, his twelve-year-old son Manasseh became king and reigned for fifty-five years.

Unfortunately for the people of Judah, Manasseh was the antithesis of his faithful father. He may have been one of the most wicked kings of all Judah, and much of his long reign corrupted the people and took them further from the God of Abraham.

The Book of 2 Chronicles details much of the destructive behavior of Manasseh. This path of destruction began when Manasseh rebuilt all the high places his father had destroyed. High places were centers of worship in the Canaanite pagan religion, so called because of their location on hills and mountains.

The chief pagan god in this scheme was Baal. Manasseh showed particular enthusiasm for Baal by erecting pillars throughout the land and building altars to him and his fellow gods in the Jerusalem temple. He practiced sorcery, divination, and other religious evils that God had prohibited for His people. He sank to new horrors as he made his own children "pass through the fire," a euphemism for offering his own flesh and blood to these gods as human sacrifice.

The prophets of Judah could not lessen Manasseh's enthusiasm for idolatry and bring him back to the God of his fathers. In fact, tradition has him killing the prophet Isaiah (his father's confidant) by having him sawn in half.

Scripture summarizes Manasseh's life with this poignant statement: "He did much evil in the sight of the Lord." His sin corrupted not only his own soul, but the nation of Judah to the point they were considered worse than the surrounding pagan nations.

Eventually Manasseh was taken captive by the Assyrians. During the affliction of his captivity, he humbled himself and sought the Lord. God heard him and restored him to his kingdom in Jerusalem. Upon restoration, he began to destroy all the pagan places of worship he had built, but unfortunately the damage to the nation was harder to undo. The people came back to the God of Israel, and rather than worshiping the pagan gods at the high places, they offered up worship to the true God in those same unsanctified spaces. It was this confusion in worship that would lead them back down into paganism in the next generation.

A modern parallel of this ancient king is the Soviet dictator Joseph Stalin. He was raised in an Orthodox family, prepared for the priesthood, yet rejected all the riches of his faith for a demonic conception of mankind. To implement this vision, he slaughtered millions of his own people, razed their places of worship, and constructed "temples" to atheistic materialism. Manasseh's repentance was just as unlikely as Stalin's would have been (except that Stalin did not repent), which shows what a miracle it truly was.

STRUCTURE OF THE PRAYER

This prayer can be divided easily into three basic parts which provide a model for all repenting people. This basic structure of praise, confession, and acts of repentance is the same found in other biblical examples of repentance, as well as in prayers of repentance found in the Orthodox Church. The glory of God leads to man seeing himself as he is, which leads to acts of change. Here is a simple outline and the text of the prayer:

I.   Praise to God for His glory & mercy toward sinners (1–7)
II.   Confession of Sin (8–10)
III. Act of Repentance (11–15)

I. O Lord Almighty, the God of our fathers, of Abraham, Isaac, and Jacob, and their righteous seed; who made heaven and earth with all their ornamentation; who set the bounds of the sea by the word of Your command; who closed the abyss and sealed it by Your fearful and glorious name; before whom all things tremble and fear because of Your power; for the majesty of Your glory is unbearable, and the wrath of Your threats toward sinners cannot be withstood; yet Your merciful promise is immeasurable and unsearchable. For You are the Lord Most High, and are tenderhearted, patient, very merciful, and repent toward the evils of man. (1-7)

II. Therefore You, O Lord God of the righteous, have not appointed repentance for the righteous, for Abraham, Isaac, and Jacob, who have not sinned against You; but You have appointed repentance for me, a sinner, because I have sinned more than the number of the sands on the seashore. My lawlessness, O Lord, is multiplied. Yes, my lawlessness is multiplied, and I am not worthy to fix my eyes to behold the heights of heaven because of the multitude of my wrongdoings. I am bent down with so many iron chains that I shake my head over my sins, neither do I have any relief. For I have provoked Your anger and done evil in Your sight. I have set up abominations and multiplied idols. (8–10)

III. Now therefore, I bow the knee of my heart, begging goodness from You. I have sinned, O Lord, I have sinned, and I know my lawlessness. I ask and beg You: forgive me, O Lord, forgive me, and do not destroy me because of my lawlessness; neither reserve evils for me, nor be wrathful forever; nor condemn me to the lowest parts of the earth; for You are the Lord God of those who repent. And in me, though I am unworthy, You will show Your goodness, and will save me according to Your great mercy. Therefore I shall praise You continually all the days of my life, for all the powers of the heavens praise You, and Yours is the glory unto the ages. Amen. (11–15)

WHAT WE CAN LEARN

The meaning of this prayer is fairly apparent even on a superficial reading. A man is pouring out his heart to God over his sin and asking to be restored to communion with Him. He praises God for His wondrous glory and mercy to sinners. Out of his remembrance and reflection on God comes forth his confession of sin; for one can only confess his sin when he beholds God in true worship. The depth of worship determines the depth of confession.

Once his sin is openly pronounced, he can then begin to change his heart in full repentance. This is not a single act but a movement toward continually embracing God's mercy. By clinging to God's mercy he will be saved and made whole. For he knows his heart and the direction he is bent, and only God's mercy will save him from himself.

At the end of the prayer, he moves back to the theme of the beginning of the passage, discussing God's glory. God's goodness and glory will be seen through Manasseh because God shows mercy to an unworthy soul. In this is an image of the Cross. God's glory is supremely manifest in the Cross of Christ. Manasseh, while not an unblemished innocent sacrifice, is crucifying himself before God. He is offering up his soul as an offering, and God receives, restores, and resurrects him in spite of his deep sinfulness.

This passage demonstrates the path of repentance. Man looks to God in His glory and magnifies Him, and the contrast between God and man in an act of worship illumines the sinfulness of man's heart, leading to repentance. For man to truly repent, he must truly worship.

Manasseh's repentance was born on Golgotha. For many Christians, each day is a day of the cross and the resurrection, and such was probably true for Manasseh after this dramatic experience. However, it was his imprisonment and deprivation that opened a crack in his soul for the grace of God to enter. The utter helplessness of his life shattered the image of a powerful king who could defy the traditions of his fathers and manipulate the darkness for his own control and satisfaction. The cross was thrust upon him, but he chose to bear it, and resurrection was to follow.

Most of us may not have such outward displays of wickedness, but inwardly we build kingdoms of darkness to protect ourselves from the fear of death.

USE IN THE CHURCH

This passage is appropriate and needful to pray and learn repentance. The Orthodox Church uses this during her service of Great Compline, which is said primarily during Lent. Within the service, the prayer is linked with both Psalm 50 (51) and Psalm 101 (102), which are great prayers of repentance.

St. Clement of Rome references a phrase from this passage in one of his epistles. In speaking of repentance and humility to the authority placed within the Church, he says that Christians should "bow the knees of your hearts."[2] This is a beautiful image of the humility of the inner man manifested in the body.

Many Church Fathers uphold Manasseh as an illustration of repentance, such as the Apostolic Constitutions, St. Jerome, St. Gregory the Theologian, St. Cyril of Jerusalem, and St. John Chrysostom. Chrysostom, in his Homily 67 on Matthew, talking about repentance, uses Manasseh as an illustration that those who are deep in sin never should despair of forgiveness, because repentance is always held out for them.[3] St. Cyril refers to Manasseh's sawing Isaiah in half thus: "If He who sawed the Prophet asunder was saved by repentance, shall not thou then, having done no such great wickedness, be saved?"[4] Manasseh gives all men great hope that no matter what sins we have committed, the way of repentance remains open, and cleansing from sin is available.

PSALM 151

The second short chapter to cover is Psalm 151. This is a small autobiographical psalm attributed to the King and Prophet David. The superscription of the psalm makes the point that it was written by David's "own hand" after he fought with Goliath. Here is the text of the psalm:

1   I was small among my brothers
    and the youngest in my father's house;
    I tended my father's sheep.

2   My hands built a musical instrument;
    my fingers tuned a lyre.

3   And who shall tell my Lord?
    The Lord Himself, He Himself hears.

---

2   St. Clement of Rome, First Epistle to the Corinthians, Chapter 57

3   St. John Chrysostom, Homilies on the Gospel of St. Matthew, Homily 67, Nicene and Post-Nicene Fathers Series 1, Vol. 10, Philip Schaff (ed.), p. 395

4   St. Cyril of Jerusalem, The Catechetical Lectures, Lecture 2:14, NPNF Series 2 Vol. 7, Philip Schaff (ed.), p. 11

4 He sent forth His Angel,
   and took me from my father's sheep;
   and he anointed me with his anointing oil.
5 My brothers were handsome and tall,
   but the Lord took no pleasure in them.
6 I went out to meet the foreigner,
   and he cursed me with his idols;
7 But I drew his own sword and beheaded him,
   and removed disgrace from the children of Israel.

This familiar story from the Old Testament is found in 1 Kingdoms (1 Samuel) 17. David was the youngest of his family and spent most of his days tending sheep, yet he volunteered to bring food to his brothers while they were in the army defending Israel against the Philistines. When David came to the front lines, he heard the giant Philistine champion, Goliath, curse Israel and her God. This was intolerable to David, and he was determined to fight Goliath by God's strength, even when everyone else cowered in fear.

King Saul tried to equip David with his own armor, but it did not fit the body or soul of a young shepherd boy. So David gathered stones for the sling that he used to protect his father's flock and marched to face the giant. Goliath laughed and cursed him as he approached. But David was determined to trust God. He loaded a stone and slung it toward Goliath. The stone struck the giant between the eyes, knocking him to the ground. David grabbed Goliath's sword and chopped off his head. Israel then rallied and went on to win victory against the Philistines.

Psalm 151 recounts this incident. David recalls being the smallest and youngest among his brothers. He also was a musician, which is evident from the great number of psalms he wrote.

Interestingly, David mentions that God sent forth His angel to anoint him. The account in 1 Kingdoms (1 Samuel) 16 is of Samuel the prophet coming to David's father, Jesse, and searching for the next king. David is brought forward only after all God has rejected all the others. David is chosen by God, and Samuel anoints him to be king.

Samuel could be the angel, because fundamentally *angel* means "messenger," and Samuel is God's messenger here. Another option is that this is referring to the Second Person of the Trinity. Many times throughout the Old Testament, the "Angel of the Lord" is mentioned, and this has been understood by the Fathers as a reference to a theophany of Jesus prior to His Incarnation. This is not to say that Samuel was the pre-incarnate Christ, but that in a spiritual way it was the person of Christ, the Anointed One, who anointed David. For from David a covenant was made and a genealogy established that led to the birth of Jesus Christ.

The word *christ* actually means "God's anointed one." In this sense David was a christ, yet he only foreshadowed the One who would come and fulfill what it meant to be King of kings and the Anointed of God. It is evident that God had His hand on David and used him to further His plan of salvation for mankind.

St. Ephrem the Syrian read this psalm as a prophecy of Christ:

> The voice of the cornet on a sudden amazed and called Thee to battle. Thou wentest up like a new David, by Thee was subdued a second Goliath. Thou wast not untried in combat, for a secret warfare day by day, Thou art waging against the Evil One. Exercise in secret is wont to attain the crown openly. Blessed be He Who chose Thee for our glory! (Hymn 18)[5]

For Jesus arose from humble origins, from being born in an animal's feeding trough to learning a trade as a carpenter's son. Yet Christ triumphed even though the devil cursed Him throughout His ministry. Christ turned the tables on the evil one, and by dying on the Cross, he bound and plundered the strong man Satan in the bowels of Hades. He crushed the head of the serpent, effectively rendering him powerless in man's eternal destiny. Christ used the giant's own sword—death—against the devil, and cut off his head. For trampling

---

5   St. Ephrem the Syrian, The Nisibene Hymns 18:6, Nicene and Post-Nicene Fathers Series 2, Volume 13, Philip Schaff (ed.), p. 188

down death by death, He brought life and removed the "disgrace" from His people.

Goliath is also an image of our sinful passions, which we are called to defeat through the power of the cross. St. Gregory the Theologian, in his oration on Holy Baptism, refers to this: "Art thou young? stand against thy passions; be numbered with the alliance in the army of God: do valiantly against Goliath."[6] We are to do war against our passions. This is the purpose of ascetical disciplines in the Church: that we might train ourselves to defeat those things within our hearts that quench the movement of God's grace within us.

Each of these short passages provides inspiration for repentance and courage to live in God's grace. Although they are small, they should not be underestimated, since upon reflection they fill the soul with zeal for God.

---

6   St. Gregory the Theologian, Oration on Holy Baptism 40:17, Nicene and Post-Nicene Fathers Series 2, Volume 7, Philip Schaff (ed.), p. 365

## CHAPTER 2

1 Ezra

BACKGROUND

The book of 1 Ezra is fraught with confusion, not because it is particularly hard to read. In fact, it is a very simple historical book and even entertaining at times. Confusion is created because it is known by many names. Often the book is referred to as Esdras, which is directly transliterated from the Greek name. Often Ezra, the Anglicized version of the name, is used.

The numbering is also problematic. In the Septuagint, the book we are discussing is known as 1 Ezra; 2 Ezra is identical to the Book of Ezra found in the Protestant canon. Yet in the Catholic Bible, 1 & 2 Ezra are equivalent to the Protestant Ezra and Nehemiah, respectively, and the book we are talking about here is listed as 3 Ezra. There is also an apocalyptic Book of Ezra that is not found in the Septuagint, but is included in the Catholic Vulgate as 4 Ezra. Are you confused yet?

The historical events covered in 1 Ezra are almost identical to those related in 2 Chronicles 35–36, 2 Ezra (Ezra), and Nehemiah. However, the focus of 1 Ezra is on the temple and liturgical worship, as opposed to the city of Jerusalem in Chronicles, or the law in Nehemiah and 2 Ezra (Ezra).

STRUCTURE

    I.   Life of Josiah. Josiah Celebrates the Passover, Battles with Egypt, & Suffers Death (1:1–31) 647 BC

    II.   The Last Days of Judah & the Babylonian Victory (1:32–55)

WHAT WE CAN LEARN

The heart of the book of 1 Ezra is chapters 3:1—5:6. This passage is often referred to as the Story of the Three Bodyguards, and the prince of Judah Zerubbabel is at the center of the story. Because of where this account is positioned in the book, it appears that the author is highlighting Zerubbabel. The teaching related in this story is a fulcrum, central to the themes of the book. Also, this story is unique to this book; it cannot be found in any of the other Old Testament historical books.

Zerubbabel is an important but somewhat mysterious figure in this phase of Jewish history. His name means "seed of Babylon," which suggests his place of origin and birth. He was part of the group of exiles living in Babylon. Whereas Daniel and his friends were young when taken as exiles, Zerubbabel was born in Babylon. The land of Babylon was all he knew outside of the tradition and stories his parents taught him concerning Zion. This is significant. Even though Zerubbabel never saw Jerusalem or worshipped in her now-destroyed Temple, his family instilled a love and longing for the Promised Land in his heart.

Zerubbabel was the son of Shealtiel, in the line of David. He was the legal successor of the former King Jeconiah. Outside of 1 Ezra, he can be found in the books of Ezra-Nehemiah, Zechariah, and Haggai with a small mention in Sirach (48:11). Zerubbabel and the high priest Joshua led the exiled remnant from Babylon to Jerusalem and rebuilt the temple. It was early in the reign of Darius Hystaspes, or Darius I (521–486), that Zerubbabel laid the cornerstone of the temple. This temple is often referred to as the Second Temple, as opposed to the destroyed Temple of Solomon.

Within the biblical account, Zerubbabel faced opposition from various groups in trying to rebuild the temple. The opposition primarily came from the Samaritan people, yet the prophet Haggai places much of the blame on the lukewarm faith of the Jewish community. Zerubbabel was also made a governor of Jerusalem under Persian authority, and because of his disappearance from Jewish history after this period, some suggest that he was called back to Persia during the latter part of his life. There are hints given in Haggai and Zechariah that he was intended to be enthroned as a king in a renewed line of David, yet this never materialized.

In 1 Ezra, Zerubbabel is found in this central story of the three bodyguards. King Darius organizes a great banquet for all the nobility and officials of his empire. Three young men who are his bodyguards propose a contest to name the strongest thing in the world. The winner, they propose, will receive authority, riches, and power from the king. The three write down their answers and place them under the king's pillow to be discovered in the morning. The king then gathers all the officers of the kingdom to listen to the answers and judge between them.

The first bodyguard says the strongest thing is wine. It can equalize all men, softens sorrows, can cause strife between friends, and brings forgetfulness of behavior. The second man says the king is strongest. The king rules over all men, he can make war, in cases of victory he gets the spoils, he levies taxes, and all men obey him.

The third bodyguard is the Jew, Zerubbabel. Rather than giving a single answer like the other bodyguards, he squeezes in a second response. He argues, "Women are strongest, but above all things the truth conquers" (3:12). Women give birth to all men and make garments for men; and men's behavior is largely motivated by the women in their lives. Perhaps he speaks first of women to capture their attention so they will listen to his argument.

Look at the other guards' responses and see the contrast between their answers and Zerubbabel's insistence on truth. The first three answers concern the material world. It seems that Zerubbabel wins this argument, and as a result of his convincing speech, he earns the right to deepen the argument to eternal rather than earthly matters.

For Zerubbabel, truth is more than an idea; truth is the Creator, for "Is not He great who made all things? For His truth is great and stronger than all things" (4:35). Truth is eternal, because all else, including wine, the king, and women, contains unrighteousness and is infected with death. Truth is the strength, the kingdom, the power, and the majesty of all ages. In benediction Zerubbabel exclaims, "Blessed is the God of Truth" (4:40).

After he finishes speaking, the people respond by shouting, "Great is the truth, for it is the strongest!" (4:41). The king proclaims Zerubbabel victorious. He asks him to rule by his side and make a request to be fulfilled. Zerubbabel asks that Jerusalem and the temple be rebuilt in accordance with the promise the former Persian king, Cyrus, had made.

Darius offers his protection and help to rebuild. He also liberates the Jews from compulsory obligations in Persia and encourages them to return to their homeland. Zerubbabel leaves the presence of the king, faces Jerusalem, and praises God, the "King of Heaven" (4:58). He proclaims that victory comes from God, the same attribute he ascribed earlier to truth. He then gives thanks and proclaims this victory to the Jews of Babylon. They rejoice and celebrate with feasting for seven days.

At this point, the book returns to the story we find in Ezra-Nehemiah. The exiles are named and return to rebuild Jerusalem and the temple.

This account and its placement within the book affirm for the Jews that it is on truth that Jerusalem and the temple were rebuilt. At the heart of their religion is truth. Not truth as an abstract Greek idea, but Truth as a Person who relates to mankind. This sense of Truth as a Person provides Christians with a foreshadowing of the Person of Christ and paints a clear image of the ultimate focus of God's revelation. It is no surprise that the Fathers quote frequently from this passage.

The picture of Christ as Truth is apparent to the Christian, but the other images in this passage also provide a source of Christology.

Wine in Scripture represents new life and transformation. When man partakes of the wine of Christ, he is united with Truth and transformed. The king suggests power and authority over all things. Christ is the King of kings, and under His rule all things are done rightly with order and result in peace and freedom.

Woman images first the Theotokos, because she was the vessel whereby Truth entered the world and became man. The order in which Zerubbabel puts his answers even prophesies that Truth will proceed from a woman. Zerubbabel's woman also typifies the Church. The Church is often spoken of as the Bride of Christ, and God has ordained that just like the Theotokos, the Church will be the vessel to communicate Truth to mankind. When man unites himself with the Church, he is uniting with Christ, for the Church is His body.

Ultimately, Truth stands above all, just as Zerubbabel proclaims. Each of these images is deficient apart from Christ, the personification of Truth. Wine becomes destructive rather than transformative. The king becomes a dictator who destroys mankind rather than bringing peace and freedom. Women "are unjust, all the children of the men and their works are unjust" (4:37). It is only when an innocent young woman submits herself to the voice of Truth and announces, "Behold the maidservant of the Lord! Let it be to me according to your word" (Luke 1:38), that Truth is manifest in the world.

USE IN THE CHURCH

Zerubbabel is seen as a type of Christ and is mentioned in both genealogies of Christ given in Matthew and Luke. His actions and Davidic lineage provide a foreshadowing of the person of Christ in the Old Testament, and the Church embraces this imagery. Because of the centrality of Truth and the glimpse of Truth as Person, the Fathers seize upon the story of the three bodyguards. This account is widely quoted by such Fathers as Ss. Athanasius, Ambrose, Ephrem the Syrian, John Chrysostom, and John of Damascus.

St. Athanasius discusses this story in the midst of his struggle with the Arian heresy. Arius claimed that Christ was a created being rather than being one essence with Father.[7] Athanasius quotes 1 Ezra 4:36 to defend the eternal Person of Jesus Christ as the eternal Truth proclaimed by Zerubbabel. He argues that Zerubbabel gained victory by upholding Truth over all things. Christ is above all things and is the Christian's victory.

Zerubbabel is commemorated on the Sunday of the Ancestors of Christ, the Sunday before the Nativity. He is also mentioned during the commemoration of the Seven Youths of Ephesus. The troparion of the feast proclaims: "The Youths surely appeared by number and by faith as honored eyes of the Church of Christ, blazing more brightly than the stone of Zerubbabel. Let us in spirit praise their godlike spirits."

This biblical reference is found within Zechariah's vision of the lampstand and the olive trees (Zech. 4). Zerubbabel wants to know the identity of these prophetic images, but before God reveals their meaning, He gives a revelation of Himself. God first says, "Not by mighty power nor by strength, but by My Spirit" (Zechariah 4:6). Whatever God is planning to accomplish in the world will not be via man alone; it will be something that can only be accomplished through God's action.

Then God calls out to someone He calls the "great mountain" and declares the ultimate work He will accomplish. God will bring forth the stone of the inheritance. The stone is Christ—in case there is any doubt as to this identity, God proclaims that "its grace equals My grace." Christ is light of light, True God of True God, as the Creed proclaims. Although Zerubbabel lays the cornerstone of the temple—and this is truly a work of God—a greater Stone is prefigured that will be the True Cornerstone and the Rock of man's salvation.

How does this relate to the memory of the Seven Youths of Ephesus? The Seven Youths were friends during the reign of the Roman Emperor Decius (AD 249–251). They were Christians and had entered military service together. The emperor arrived in Ephesus demanding public worship and sacrifice to idols. The Seven

---

7   St. Athanasius, Against the Arians, Discourse 2, 16:20. Nicene and Post-Nicene Fathers Series 2, Volume 4, Philip Schaff (ed.), p. 359

refused and were stripped of their military ranks and privileges.

Before they could be martyred, they fled to the surrounding mountains and hid in a cave. There they waited to be found and martyred. The emperor discovered their whereabouts, but rather than openly martyr them, he sealed the entrance to their cave, dooming them to a fate of starvation. Some of the dignitaries at the sealing were secretly Christians, and they came back to attach a metal plaque to the cave detailing the names and fate of these young Christians.

Miraculously, the Lord placed them into a deep sleep, preserving them from death. Two centuries later, after persecutions ceased and during the reign of Christian Emperor Theodosius the Younger (AD 408–450), a heretical group was growing that denied the general resurrection of the dead at the Second Coming of Christ. These Seven Youths became instrumental in resolving this conflict.

The owner of the land around the cave discovered the sealed entrance and had his workers open the cave. The Sleepers were awakened, and their bodies and clothes had experienced no decay. Not realizing the passing of time, the young men prepared themselves to be martyred. One secretly left the cave to buy bread for the others and was amazed that those in town spoke of Christ openly.

After trying to pay for bread with ancient money, he was detained and taken to the Bishop of Ephesus. The bishop listened to his story and went to the cave along with others from the city. There they found the young men and the plaque describing their imprisonment in the cave.

After meeting the men, the bishop declared that this was a sign from God proclaiming the general resurrection from the dead. Soon the word spread, and the emperor arrived to meet the youths. During this meeting, in front of all present, the youths lay down and fell asleep until the general resurrection.

The "stone of Zerubbabel" was a type that proclaimed the Person of Christ in the midst of the seven candlesticks, which represent the people of God. The Seven Youths are also seven lamps whose life manifests the Truth of Christ and the resurrection more brightly than the dim figures of the Old Testament.

First Ezra retells the story of the people of God rebuilding their lives after exile and persecution. Central to the foundation of this reconstruction is Truth. Christians who read this book today should be able to see the centrality of Christ and His Cross as foundational to the life of faith.

## CHAPTER 3

Tobit

BACKGROUND AND SUMMARY

Tobit is the account of a righteous Jew who lived among pagans and unfaithful Jews, yet continued to be faithful to the God of Israel. His story takes place after the Assyrian takeover of the Northern Kingdom of Israel in 720 BC. Tobit was a member of the tribe of Naphtali, who lived around the Sea of Galilee. This northern tribe was largely idolatrous during this period, and this led to their destruction by Assyria. However, not all were corrupt. Tobit was an exception; he went to Jerusalem every year to offer sacrifices and pay his tithes.

After the invasion of Assyria, Tobit is taken to the city of Nineveh with many other Israelites. There he continues to behave righteously by giving alms and showing mercy to those in need. He even gives illegal burial to those of his countrymen who have been cruelly killed by the king. This ultimately leads to the confiscation of his property, which leaves him, his wife, and his son Tobias destitute and homeless.

A new king arises among the Assyrians, so Tobit is able to move back to Nineveh and continue his former habit of philanthropy. After one of his trips of mercy, he comes home exhausted and collapses outside his dwelling. While he is asleep, droppings from birds fall into his eyes and blind him. As a result of the blindness, he falls into poverty. His wife is less than sympathetic with his plight. She asks in frustration at their situation, "Are your acts of charity and righteous deeds lawful? Behold, you are a know-it-all!" (2:14).

Even at that dark hour, God is preparing a way of salvation for Tobit. In another city in another part of the kingdom, one of his distant relatives is suffering as well. A man named Raguel and his wife Edna are having problems with their daughter, Sarah. An evil spirit is killing every man who becomes her husband. The demon Asmodeus ("Creature of Judgment") has killed seven bridegrooms in turn, each before his marriage could be consummated. Rather than sympathizing with her, the household servants are accusing Sarah of causing the deaths.

One day Tobit remembers that he has lent a great deal of money to a man named Gabael. He asks his son to go to Gabael and ask for the money, and while there to see the family of Raguel. A mysterious man named Azariah ("The Lord Helps") appears and offers to act as guide for Tobias on his journey. Azariah is actually the Archangel Raphael in disguise. Tobias follows him, and on the journey they stop at the River Tigris and miraculously catch a fish. Raphael instructs Tobias to gut the fish but to keep the heart, liver, and gall bladder.

They make it to the house of Raguel, and seeing the sorrow of the family, Tobias bravely asks Sarah to be his wife at the advice of Raphael. Raphael tells him not to fear, but to cense the wedding chamber with the burning fish parts in order to exorcise the demon. During the night, Raguel, the father-in-law, digs a grave for Tobias. He is amazed to see Tobias come out of the house alive the next day. Tobias then finds Gabael and receives the money owed to his father Tobit.

Tobias and Sarah depart for home to be with Tobias's parents. Once home, Raphael instructs Tobias to anoint his father's eyes with the remaining fish parts. Tobit is healed and there is great joy in the family. Raphael reveals who he is, the men praise God, and Tobit offers a beautiful prayer to God.

WHAT WE CAN LEARN

This book is full of moral wisdom and is used as such by many of the Fathers of the Church. The life of Tobit illustrates a variety of virtues that should flow from the life of the righteous. Good works, prayer, fasting, care for the dead, and marital love are but some of the virtues exemplified. Yet it is the power of almsgiving that dominates the vision of the Fathers in their use of this book.

Before sending his son Tobias off on his journey, Tobit gives parting wisdom designed to strengthen and uphold him in whatever circumstances he may encounter. Tobit is quick to instill in his son those precepts that will enable him to remain faithful to the God of Israel and protect him from the influence of the pagan world. The circumstances create an urgency of message and point to the importance of this parting advice.

> Do almsgiving from your possessions to all who do righteousness. When you do almsgiving, do not let your eye be envious. Do not turn your face away from any poor man, so the face of God will not be turned away from you. Do almsgiving based on the quantity of your possessions. If you possess only a few, do not be afraid to give according to the little you have. You are storing up a good treasure for yourself in the day of necessity. For almsgiving delivers us from death and prevents us from entering into the darkness. Indeed, almsgiving is a good gift for all who do it before the Most High. . . . From your bread, give to him who is hungry, and from your clothing, give to the naked. If you have more than you need, do almsgiving, and do not let your eye envy the almsgiving when you do it. (Tobit 4:7–10, 16)

Of all the things a father could tell a son before he wanders out into the world, Tobit's overriding advice is generosity of spirit and care for one's fellowman. Tobit's instructions on almsgiving teach that we should give to the needy. Our giving should not be done grudgingly but with a generous heart. Almsgiving is to be sacrificial, for he instructs those with little to give as well as those with much. The Gospels reinforce this same teaching as critical to spiritual growth. Jesus' praise of the impoverished widow giving her last mite is evidence of the importance of this virtue.

Part of the sacrifice of giving is that it is an act of worship to God. This explains why almsgiving and prayer are linked, for the sacrifice of alms is a physical manifestation of worship, while prayer is a spiritual act. Almsgiving acts as a physical prayer, and God promises to hear because it comes from a sacrificial and righteous heart. Almsgiving also delivers from death and stores up treasure in heaven for the day of judgment. Giving of alms is a victory blow against the fear of death. It is confidence in the life-giving grace of God against the specter of deprivation.

Tobit's life exemplified the virtues he proclaimed to his son. In the very beginning of the story, we see Tobit giving a tithe. He gave a tenth of his harvest to the Levites serving in Jerusalem. A second tenth he spent when he journeyed to Jerusalem for festal worship. The third tenth he gave to those who were in need. This was not done as a perfunctory obedience to the law, but sacrificially and out of a heart of gratitude and trust in his God. Later in chapter 1, we see that his acts of charity are the very things that bring about the rest of the events of the book. The pagan king is determined to stop Tobit through persecution. Even Tobit's wife is not convinced of the virtue of charity because of the awful results it seems to produce in their lives.

Later in the book, the Archangel Raphael vindicates the instructions given by Tobit when he reveals himself and shows his own actions as an answer to Tobit's prayer.

> Prayer is good with fasting, almsgiving, and righteousness. A few prayers with righteousness are better than many with wrongdoing. It is better to do almsgiving than to lay up gold. For almsgiving rescues one from death, and it will wash away every sin. Those who do almsgiving and are righteous will be full of life. But those who sin are enemies of their own life. (Tobit 12:8–10)

Raphael has just revealed himself, and you can imagine the surprise of the men. Tobit is beginning to see that the prayers he offered to God were answered in ways he could not have imagined. Even though Raphael makes note of his prayers, he is quick to mention that not prayer alone, but the alms, fasting, and righteous life of Tobit led to the answer. Then he reaffirms Tobit's counsel to his son that giving of alms is better than earthly gold, because it is treasure laid up in heaven. Alms once again are seen as life-giving and as a protection against death and its encroaching darkness.

Almsgiving delivers from death because it is an act of crucifixion. It is an embrace of the cross in which you die to yourself, unite with the Author of life, and experience resurrection. Yet almsgiving is not cruciform if done selfishly and grudgingly; it must flow from a heart of sacrifice and trust in the Giver of life. It should be no surprise that almsgiving along with prayer and fasting is extolled by the Church, especially during Great Lent, when we are walking with the Church to the cross in order to experience the joy of resurrection.

USE IN THE CHURCH

The New Testament is replete with instructions on almsgiving, prayer, and fasting that are strikingly similar to those in Tobit. Matthew 6:1–18; Luke 6:30; 2 Corinthians 8:12; 9:7; Galatians 6:10; and Hebrews 13:1–3 are some passages that teach Tobit's virtues. The passage in Hebrews reminds Christians to be hospitable to strangers because they may be entertaining angels unawares. This is usually taken to refer to Abraham entertaining the "three men," but it may also be a reference to Tobias's befriending of the Archangel Raphael.

Christ is seen in the Book of Tobit. Tobit himself is an image of Christ. He is a righteous innocent, suffering only to be redeemed from death to life. Even more strikingly, Tobias images Christ's march to the Cross, descent into Hades, defeat of the devil, and victorious Resurrection.

When Tobias met his future bride, he knew the story and fate of her previous seven husbands, yet this did not deter his purpose. He strode bravely into the gravelike bridal chamber to meet and defeat the demon. None of the bride's family expected him to return, but he emerged victorious and joyful from the bridal chamber the next morning. In doing so, he brought joy to all and cause for feasting. This is reminiscent of hymns we sing of Christ during Pascha: "Rejoice, O Jerusalem, for thou hast seen Christ the king come forth from the tomb like a bridegroom in procession," and "As from a bridal chamber hath Christ shone forth."

Tobias sometimes appears in the Church's iconography. In some stand-alone icons of the Archangel Raphael, Tobias carries a fish and holds the angel's right hand. In his left hand Raphael holds a vessel with healing medicine, for his name means "God who heals."

The Fathers often refer to Tobit in speaking of almsgiving and other virtues. Polycarp, the Shepherd of Hermas, Chrysostom, Ambrose, Leo the Great, and Gregory the Great all refer to Tobit in their discussion on the power of almsgiving and fasting. The two virtues seem inseparable in the mind of the Fathers. Giving alms is a form of laying your treasure up in heaven. St. Cyprian compares Tobit to the longsuffering Job, who endures affliction yet maintains his righteousness. The similarity between the wives of both men is striking.[8] Within the pages of Tobit is also an inverse form of the Golden Rule, which Chrysostom quotes in one of his sermons.[9] The rule is found in 4:15, where Tobit gives his parting wisdom to Tobias as the son begins his journey: "What you yourself hate, do not do to anyone."

We have an extant commentary from a British Father of the Church—the Venerable Bede (672–735). Bede's intent in this commentary is not just to provide a cursory retelling of Tobit or to point out moral application of the text, but to show forth Christ. He does this by looking at the images or types in the book and how those types are fulfilled in the life of the Church and salvation history.

One specific example is his commentary on the fish Tobias and Raphael caught. This fish was eventually instrumental in the resurrection of the story. It destroyed the power of the demon that oppressed the future wife of Tobias, and brought sight back to righteous Tobit.

---

8   St. Cyprian, Three Books of Testimonies against the Jews, Book Three, Of the Benefit of Good Works and Mercy. Ante-Nicene Fathers, Volume 5, Philip Schaff (ed.), p. 531

9   St. John Chrysostom, The Homilies on the Statutes to the People of Antioch, Homily 13:7. Nicene and Post Nicene Fathers, Series 1, Volume 9, Philip Schaff (ed.), p. 428

Bede looks at this fish as an image of the devil. At first, the fish sought to devour Tobias, yet he caught it and gutted it in on dry land for all to see. Tobias then becomes a type of Christ, as Bede teaches: "The Lord seized hold of the devil and by dying caught and conquered the one who wanted to catch Him in death."[10] Later when Tobias burns the innards of the fish as incense to drive away the demon, Bede sees the burning of the fish as equivalent to the renouncing of the devil at baptism. For in destroying the "life" of the fish, the power the devil held over Tobias's bride was broken. Bede's commentary continually illuminates and shows Christ as manifest, teaching us today how to read Scripture through the light of Christ.

The Book of Tobit truly is full of wisdom and provides an example of a righteous man who clings to his God regardless of his circumstances. The prayers recorded in the book are beautiful and make for excellent additions to the devotional life of any believer. The light of Christ shines forth through this man and his son, as both become types of Christ through His Cross and Resurrection. Their willingness to lay down life ultimately results in resurrection.

---

10   Bede: On Tobit and on the Canticle of Habakkuk. Translated by Sean Connolly. Dublin: Four Courts Press, 1997, p. 48

 *Judith*

Occasionally a story comes along that is full of such surprise and power it leaves an imprint that forces you to change the way you think and act. Judith is such a story.

The Book of Judith contains a mix of historical peoples and places. Because of this compilation of traditional Jewish enemies and geographical oddities, it has created discomfort for many who try to fit it into a consistent historical framework. From the first verse strange things are happening. The Babylonian King Nebuchadnezzar is in the twelfth year of his reign in the city of Nineveh. Any Jewish reader would know that Nebuchadnezzar's father destroyed Nineveh in his conquest of the Assyrians. This should tip us off that the author of Judith is doing something different here. Judith may best be understood as a parable or work of historical fiction designed to instill certain virtues and teach certain truths to the readers of this story.

Judith can be divided into two portions. The first section describes the actions of Nebuchadnezzar's general, Holofernes (chapters 1–7). The second section introduces and highlights the Jewish heroine Judith (chapters 8–16). Within the book, a stark contrast is laid out between the cruel and pagan general Holofernes, the Ammonite Achior, and the godly Judith. Although a woman, she is the heroine of this story and showed great courage that no man in her city could equal. St. Jerome calls her actions "manly."

The story begins when Nebuchadnezzar appoints a general named Holofernes to help conquer and annihilate any people who dare to resist him. Holofernes comes to Judea, but the people, under the leadership of Uzziah, fortify themselves in the mountains to resist. Holofernes then asks one of his commanders, Achior of the Ammonites, who these people are. Achior gives a version of Israel's history and says:

> "Yet now they have come back to their God and returned from their dispersion, and they have taken back Jerusalem, where their sanctuary is. They have settled in the hill country, for it was not inhabited. Now my lord and master, if there is any sin of ignorance in this people and they sin against their God, then we will identify their offense and will go up to defeat them. But if there is no lawlessness in their nation, then let my lord leave them alone, lest their Lord shield them, and their God defend them, and we will become a reproach before the whole earth." (Judith 5:19–21)

This angers Holofernes, and he proclaims that he will destroy the Jews (6:2). He launches his campaign against them, capturing their water source, which causes suffering and death for the people. In the face of thirst, the people are ready to surrender, but Uzziah encourages them to hope that God will intervene. He does this in an unexpected way.

A woman named Judith lives in the town that is being besieged. She is a widow who has lived a life of chastity and prayer. She is also rich, young, and beautiful. Judith invites Uzziah and the officers to her house and recommends a state of repentance be declared for five days. During this time of repentance, she asks that the gates be opened so that she can go out and meet Holofernes. She does so, wearing her most beautiful clothes and jewelry.

The officers of Holofernes meet her, and she tells them she has a great secret to tell that will allow Holofernes to conquer Judea. Dazzled by her beauty, he lets her speak and provides her with her own tent. After three days, he holds a lavish banquet for her. At the banquet, Holofernes becomes drunk, staggers into bed, and falls asleep. While he is sleeping, Judith finds his sword and chops off his head.

She places it in a food bag and leaves the camp to return to her village.

When she arrives in the city, the people rejoice and hang Holofernes' head on the city walls. Then they attack the enemy. Having been victorious, the Jews offer sacrifices to God and honor Judith. The story ends with Judith offering a beautiful song of thanksgiving that recounts the goodness of God and His protection of the weak and powerless. As expected, many men desire to become her husband, but she remains a widow and lives a life of chastity and prayer.

In the Book of Judges there is a very similar story to that of Judith which is worth comparing. This is the story of Deborah, Barak, and Jael, found in Judges 4. Early in the history of Israel, between the entry into the Promised Land and the rise of the monarchy, pagans had begun to oppress the people of Israel, and God called forth a prophetess by the name of Deborah. She approached a man named Barak to deliver Israel from the enemy and their evil general Sisera. Barak was frightened and refused to do it unless Deborah accompanied him. As a result, she prophesied that he would receive no honor for this victory, but Sisera would be delivered into the hands of a woman.

Sisera was routed by Barak in battle and fled to more friendly territory. He pitched his tent near an assumed ally and was greeted with hospitality by the ally's wife, Jael. After Sisera had eaten, he lay down for a nap, and Jael entered his tent with a tent peg and hammer. She nailed the peg through the side of his head. This sealed the victory of Israel over her enemies. Deborah and Barak then rejoiced and sang a song of praise to God, which included accolades to Jael for her courageous actions. Such accounts in Scripture continually remind us that God often uses the weak and unexpected to deliver His people. His ways are not our ways, and His thoughts are not our thoughts.

WHAT WE CAN LEARN

The Fathers of the Church use Judith in various ways. It should come as no surprise that her faithful chastity in widowhood provides a model of virtue extolled by many of the Fathers. It was not just her chastity that was exemplary, but her life of prayer, whereby her chastity was a physical expression of her life of devotion to God. In the Book of Judith the Fathers see a picture and example of the cross, the power of prayer in a pure life, a type of the Church, a model of humility, and an image of God's protection of the weak and oppressed.

Judith is an image of crucifixion, risking death in order to experience resurrection. Judith is introduced to the reader in chapter 8. She knows what is happening to her people and their desire to surrender to the enemy. Because of their lack of water, they speak angrily to their leaders for not giving in to Holofernes. The rulers cave under the pressure, but not wanting full surrender, they compromise by asking the people to wait five days for God to act and deliver them.

Judith sees this as testing God. She upbraids the leaders for their actions and encourages them to trust in God regardless of the outcome. Calling to mind all the times past that God delivered Israel in the face of great testing, she says, "For [God] has not tested us with the fire, even as He did them, to search out their hearts. Nor has He punished us. Rather, the Lord scourges those drawing near to Him as a warning" (Judith 8:27). Clement of Alexandria quotes this verse, or perhaps a proverb based on the verse, like this: "Whoever is near the Lord is full of stripes."[11] Judith knows that those faithful to God have to endure some hardship to experience God's glory. She may not have called it resurrection, but this was the outcome of all the faithful endurance those before her experienced. Crucifixion is central to the Christian experience, and the closer to God we become, the deeper our experience of the Cross of Christ.

Judith was not fearful of death merely from her knowledge of Israel's history; she had experienced this knowledge by being crucified through her widowhood. For when her husband died, she set up a tent on her rooftop, clothed herself in sackcloth, and wore garments of widowhood. For a little over three years, she managed her husband's property while living a life of fasting and prayer, leaving her house only to deliver the people from destruction. She was dead

11   Clement of Alexandria, The Stromata, or the Miscellanies, Book 2, Chapter 7, Ante-Nicene Fathers, Volume 2, Philip Schaff (ed.), p. 355

to the world, and freedom from the fear of death gave her power. St. Ambrose comments, "For she trembled not at the danger of death, nor even at the danger her modesty was in . . . she feared not the blow of one scoundrel, nor even the weapons of a whole army . . . as one looks at her overwhelming danger, one would say she went out to die; as one looks at her faith, one says she went out to fight."[12]

She is an example not only of the power of the cross, but also of the power of prayer in a pure life. She lived a life of chastity with fasting and prayer. It was this life of purity that enlarged her prayer and gave her wisdom and faith to trust God so completely that she could become a sacrifice to deliver her people.

St. Ambrose addresses her purity through temperance in a treatise on widowhood. For Ambrose, Judith is an example of a faithful and righteous widow. He mentions her temperance, chastity, fasting, and prayer as reasons for her triumph over the evil Holofernes. He highlights her virtue of temperance as cause for her cutting off the head of the drunken general, rather than letting the drunkenness of wine lead her into his adulterous arms. St. Jerome praises her purity when he writes a letter to a recently widowed Christian noblewoman:

> You have widows like yourself worthy to be your models, Judith renowned in Hebrew story and Anna the daughter of Phanuel famous in the gospel. Both these lived day and night in the temple and preserved the treasure of their chastity by prayer and by fasting. One was a type of the Church which cuts off the head of the devil, as Judith cut off the head of Holofernes, and the other first received in her arms the Savior of the world and had revealed to her the holy mysteries which were to come.[13]

---

12 St. Ambrose, On the Duties of Clergy, Book 3, Chapter 13:83, Nicene and Post-Nicene Fathers Series 2, Volume 10, Philip Schaff (ed.), p. 81

13 St. Jerome, The Letters of St. Jerome, To Salvina, Letter 29:9, Nicene and Post-Nicene Fathers Series 2, Volume 6, Philip Schaff (ed.), p. 168

Judith's pure life enabled her to conquer the enemy, and in doing so she is compared with the Theotokos as a type of the Church. Just as the purity of the Church enables her to overcome the evil one, so did Judith conquer Holofernes; and by purity of life the Theotokos received the Savior into her womb, as does the Church when receiving the Holy Mysteries.

Judith is also a type of Christ. She is a godly innocent woman who lived a life of prayer and virtue. Then when the moment arises to save her people, she marches into the very gates of Hades. In the bowels of the grave, she cuts off the head of the enemy, as Christ descended into Hades and crushed the head of the serpent. Christ destroyed the power of the devil over mankind, thereby delivering man from death to life. Judith comes out of the enemy camp of death with the head of the oppressor. The people rejoice because they have been brought from death to life. You can imagine the shock and relief many of the people felt when she came back to the city. Surely they expected her dead, never to return, with a rabid Holofernes breathing fire down upon their city in revenge. We should not be surprised at the rejoicing that followed.

Judith's humility inspired her people and helped them trust their God once more. She gave them courage to defeat their enemies, and upon the victory they feasted and worshipped God for thirty days before the temple in Jerusalem. Her humility made it evident that it was not by her strength, but by her faith in the Most High, that the enemy was defeated. St. Ambrose again praises her actions and the result they had in upbraiding her people:

> Judith then followed the call of virtue, and as she follows that, she wins great benefits. It was virtuous to prevent the people of the Lord from giving themselves up to the heathen; to prevent them from betraying their native rites and mysteries, or from yielding up their consecrated virgins, their venerable widows, and modest matrons to barbarian impurity, or from ending the siege by surrender. It was virtuous for her to be willing to encounter danger on behalf of all, so as to deliver

all from danger. How great must have been the power of her virtue, which she, a woman, should claim to give counsel on the chiefest matters and not leave it in the hands of the leaders of the people! How great, again, the power of her virtue to reckon for certain upon God to help her! How great her grace to find His help![14]

Her humility not only inspired her people toward faith and righteousness, but affirmed the consistent biblical message that God resists the proud and upholds the humble and weak. The weak and humble are powerful through the power of God. St. Ambrose comments on this feature as well:

And yet she was not so elated by this success, though she might well rejoice and exult by right of her victory, as to give up the exercises of her widowhood, but refusing all who desired to wed her she laid aside her garments of mirth and took again those of her widowhood, not caring for the adornments of her triumph, thinking those things better whereby vices of the body are subdued than those whereby the weapons of an enemy are overcome.[15]

We can sympathize with the people when we consider the apparent folly of thinking that not only a woman but a widow would deliver them. Surely the people expected some great deliverer or powerful warrior to ride in and save them. Or perhaps God would send a dramatic whirlwind or earthquake to smite the enemies. Yet He chose one lowly among the people.

This seems to be how God works throughout Scripture, and it should be no surprise that even today the most humble are used by

---

14   St. Ambrose, On the Duties of Clergy, Book 3, Chapter 13:84, Nicene and Post-Nicene Fathers Series 2, Volume 10, Philip Schaff (ed.), p. 81

15   St. Ambrose, Concerning Widows, Chapter 7:42, Nicene and Post-Nicene Fathers Series 2, Volume 10, Philip Schaff (ed.), p. 81

God. You only have to read the lives of the saints and martyrs for this to become clear. In the history of the Church, even those born to nobility had to humble themselves in order to be exalted. After the victory, Judith demonstrated her humility once again. She gave the spoils of war as offerings in Jerusalem. She never remarried, but continued in her widowhood, praying and fasting as if none of these miraculous events had happened.

Judith is beloved by many Fathers of the Church, and it should be obvious why they cherished this story. It demonstrates the power of a life of virtue and the willingness to pick up the cross and face death by trusting in resurrection. Even today, we are constantly called to carry our cross and deny ourselves. Some experience this more painfully than others, yet the outcome is the same: transformation into the likeness of our Lord and the experience of His paschal joy.

 *Esther*

The Book of Esther should be familiar to most Christians. It is a dramatic story, like other books among the Readables that feature a female heroine. Esther is included in everyone's canon of Scripture. However, over the years many have questioned its fitness to be in there, because in the Hebrew version God is never mentioned. This is a somewhat unfair criticism, because it is obvious that God is present and working, even though no prayers are offered to Him and the author never mentions His name.

The absence of God is not a problem in the Septuagint version of Esther. The beginning of chapter 1 and parts of chapters 3, 4, 5, 8, and 10 are additions to the story found only in the Greek version. Many of these passages include prayers by Mordecai and Esther. At the beginning of the book, Mordecai has a vision that serves as a prologue to the events of the book, and in the last chapter this dream is interpreted and understood. In many Bibles that include these passages, they are placed as an appendix at the end of the Hebrew version. Orthodox Bibles include the text seamlessly as it occurs, but notate the verses by letters rather than numbers, such as chapter 1, verse 1a, b, c, etc.

The story of Esther takes place during the early years of the Persian Empire, not long after the Babylonian Empire had fallen, sometime around 450 BC. Jews who had been deported from Israel along with their descendants were still living in Babylon and the surrounding area. In fact, today one of the largest Jewish communities is in Iran (which is modern-day Persia), and the tomb of Mordecai and Esther is located there as well.

The story begins with Mordecai's dream, which is unique to the Septuagint. Mordecai is introduced as a "great man who served in the court of the king" (1:1b). His dream begins with the noise of thunder and earthquake, which comes from two great dragons readying themselves for combat. At the sound of the dragons' roar, the nations gather for war against the just and the unjust. The righteous nation is anxious, full of fear, and prepares for death and crying out to God. At their cry a small spring bubbles from the earth and becomes a great river. Light shines, the sun rises, and the lowly righteous "were exalted and devoured the esteemed" (1:1j).

Mordecai awakes and ponders the dream throughout the night. The next morning Mordecai overhears a plot to destroy the king and informs him of the conspiracy. The king honors Mordecai and asks him to serve in the court. The villain Haman is jealous of Mordecai's position and begins to scheme against Mordecai and his people.

The scene shifts to the palace. King Artaxerxes calls a banquet, and his queen Vashti refuses to attend. He is counseled to remove her as queen, because if the noblewomen hear of her insubordination they will rebel against their husbands. The king rids himself of Vashti and holds a beauty contest to choose a new queen. The Jewish orphan Esther, who was reared by her uncle Mordecai, enters the contest. However, Mordecai warns Esther to keep her heritage and religion a secret. Esther is chosen as queen, and Mordecai uncovers another plot to kill the king. This time the king records Mordecai's actions but does not reward him.

Haman returns, is exalted, and becomes the right-hand man of the king, but hates Mordecai because Mordecai would not bow to him like all the others in the king's court. Haman's arrogance stirs him to devise a scheme to kill Mordecai and all Jews. He drafts an order of genocide and tricks the king into signing the law to exterminate the Jews. The actual decree is included in the Septuagint version and details the extent of the genocide that Haman is planning. All Jewish women and children are to be killed as well as the men.

Mordecai and all the Jews fast and mourn over the decree. Mordecai seeks Esther's help in subverting the law. Esther balks out of fear, but promises to approach the king if Mordecai and the other Jews join her in fasting and praying. The prayers of Mordecai and Esther are recorded, which again is unique to the Septuagint. These prayers are typical of prayers found throughout Scripture. They are full of praise, petition, and even repentance of sin as Esther confesses that the Jews have dabbled with the foreign gods of their enemies.

Esther goes before the king in fear, asking that she might throw a banquet in his honor. Meanwhile, Haman secretly begins to build a gallows for Mordecai. After the banquet, insomnia grips the king, so during the night he reads the court records. He is reminded of Mordecai's good deeds and prepares to reward him. The next day he asks Haman how to reward a man he wishes to honor. Haman thinks the king is referring to himself and crafts an elaborate ceremony, which ends up honoring Mordecai. Mordecai is celebrated among all the people, while Haman seethes with jealousy.

Esther throws a second banquet and requests that she and her people be spared extermination. The king sees through Haman's deception and hangs him on the gallows he had prepared for Mordecai. Artaxerxes also sends a letter throughout the land stating that Haman's decree was to be revoked. The Jews were given the authority to follow their own religious customs with a certain level of self-governance. The copy of this decree is preserved in the Septuagint. The Feast of Purim is instituted to remember the deliverance of the Jews, and is observed by all Jews up to this day.

An epilogue ends with an interpretation of Mordecai's dream. The small spring that becomes a river is Esther. The two dragons are Mordecai and Haman. The nations gathering together for war are the Gentiles. The Jews cry out in fear, and God raises Esther to deliver her people from destruction.

WHAT WE CAN LEARN

Esther is not used liturgically in the Church and is not quoted in the New Testament, yet the Fathers of the Church find much value in this story, and their comments give insight into the teaching it holds for the Church. Their comments can be condensed into several categories, which include the need to rejoice at God's deliverance, the power of prayer and fasting, and the humility of Esther. Also, both Esther and Mordecai are held up as types of Gospel truth, revealing Christ and aspects of His Person and ministry.

By the book's end, the Jews are rejoicing at their deliverance from destruction. For this we can be thankful as well, because from this stock of humanity the Savior of all mankind arose. Not only did the people rejoice and defeat their enemies, but a perpetual feast was proclaimed that forever would celebrate Esther and their deliverance from evil. St. Athanasius, in one of his many Paschal letters sent out to inform the people of the start of the Great Fast in preparation for Pascha, refers to this celebration of Purim.

> Thus anciently, the people of the Jews, when they came out of affliction into a state of ease, kept the feast, staging a song of praise for their victory. So also the people in the time of Esther, because they were delivered from the edict of death, kept a feast to the Lord, reckoning it a feast, returning thanks to the Lord, and praising Him for having changed their condition. Therefore let us, performing our vows to the Lord, and confessing our sins, keep the feast to the Lord, in conversation, moral conduct, and manner of life; praising our Lord, Who hath chastened us a little, but hath not utterly failed nor forsaken us, nor altogether kept silence from us.[16]

Many Christians during the time of Athanasius would have been familiar with the celebration of Purim because of the Jewish population in Alexandria, and because Purim occurred near the start of Great Lent each year. So just as the ancient Jews celebrated Purim because of deliverance from extermination, Christians have reason to celebrate as well. Christ has fulfilled the image of which Esther is but a shadow. Mankind was tricked into the jaws of death through

---

16   St. Athanasius, Festal Letter 10:11. Nicene and Post-Nicene Fathers Series 2, Volume 4, Philip Schaff (ed.), p. 528

the beguiling serpent in the garden. At the proper time, Christ came to deliver man from destruction and from the tyrant who held man in bondage through the power of death. Therefore, as St. Athanasius exhorts, we should prepare ourselves, confess our sin, and keep the feast of the Lord with a song of praise for the victory given in Christ.

Athanasius mentions Esther again in another Paschal letter. This time he emphasizes the power of prayer and fasting found in the book.

It is well, my beloved, to proceed from feast to feast; again festal meetings, again holy vigils arouse our minds, and compel our intellect to keep vigil unto contemplation of good things. Let us not fulfill these days like those that mourn, but, by enjoying spiritual food, let us seek to silence our fleshly lusts. For by these means we shall have strength to overcome our adversaries, like blessed Judith when having first exercised herself in fastings and prayers, she overcame the enemies, and killed Holofernes. And blessed Esther, when destruction was about to come on all her race, and the nation of Israel was ready to perish, defeated the fury of the tyrant by no other means than by fasting and prayer to God, and changed the ruin of her people into safety.[17]

For Athanasius' flock, Great Lent is about to begin and Christians will begin fasting, praying, and holding vigils in preparation for the celebration of the Resurrection. The disciplines that are going to be undertaken in Lent are not inspired by some sense of morbid asceticism, but are spiritual exercises designed to help Christians become more united with Christ in His death, so that they may more fully celebrate His Resurrection.

Athanasius gives the examples of Judith and Esther. Judith, as we have already seen, was victorious due to her life of prayer and

---

17   St. Athanasius, Festal Letter 4:2. Nicene and Post-Nicene Fathers Series 2, Volume 4, Philip Schaff (ed.), p. 516

fasting; and Esther does the same in the face of death. She enters a time of fasting and prayer to strengthen her will and heart to defend her people from evil. This same cycle occurs each year for Christians as our hearts are strengthened in asceticism to rejoice in Christ, who has trampled down death by death.

Esther is also an example of humility, which draws the grace of God into our hearts. St. Clement of Rome, an early bishop of Rome, wrote an epistle to the Corinthian church around AD 95 in which he references the prayer of Esther and her humility.

> Esther also, being perfect in faith, exposed herself to no less danger, in order to deliver the twelve tribes of Israel from impending destruction. For with fasting and humiliation she entreated the everlasting God, who seeth all things; and He, perceiving the humility of her spirit, delivered the people for whose sake she had encountered peril.[18]

Like Athanasius above, he recognizes Esther's prayer and fasting, but it is due to her humility that God heard her prayer and through her delivered the people of Israel. A humble heart reflects the heart of God and unites us with Him, so that what we ask in prayer is what God desires. Esther was such a person.

Esther is seen by the Fathers as both a type of the Church and a type of Christ. St. Jerome says, "Esther, a type of the church, frees her people from danger and, after having slain Haman whose name means iniquity, hands down to posterity a memorable day and a great feast."[19] The Church is Christ's Body and thereby the vehicle that God uses to spread His salvation throughout the world. In this way, Esther too was the vessel whereby God saved His people. Like Jesus, she walked into the mouth of death to defeat the death of her people. St. Ambrose illustrates this truth:

---

18 St. Clement of Rome, 1 Epistle to the Corinthians 55, Ante-Nicene Fathers, Volume 1, Philip Schaff (ed.), p. 20

19 St. Jerome, The Letters of St. Jerome, To Paulinus, Letter 53:8, Nicene and Post-Nicene Fathers Series 2, Volume 6, Philip Schaff (ed.), p. 101

Why did Queen Esther expose herself to death and not fear the wrath of a fierce king? Was it not to save her people from death, an act both seemly and virtuous? The king of Persia himself also, though fierce and proud, yet thought it seemly to show honor to the man who had given information about a plot which had been laid against himself, to save a free people from slavery, to snatch them from death, and not to spare him who had pressed on such unseemly plans. So finally he handed over to the gallows the man that stood second to himself, and whom he counted chief among all his friends, because he considered that he had dishonored him by his false counsels.[20]

She saved a people from slavery and snatched them from death, just as Christ has done for us.

Mordecai typifies Christ, for through his persecutions he shares in the sufferings of Christ and in a sense becomes a type of Christ. St. Aphrahat (a Persian saint) lists multiple ways in which Mordecai was an image of Christ, and in doing so echoes St. Jerome in demonstrating Esther as a type of the Church.

Mordecai also was persecuted as Jesus was persecuted. Mordecai was persecuted by the wicked Haman; and Jesus was persecuted by the rebellious People. Mordecai by his prayer delivered his people from the hands of Haman; and Jesus by His prayer delivered His people from the hands of Satan. Mordecai was delivered from the hands of his persecutor; and Jesus was rescued from the hands of His persecutors. Because Mordecai sat and clothed himself with sackcloth, he saved Esther and his people from the sword; and because Jesus clothed Himself with a body and was illuminated, He saved the Church and her children from death. Because of

---

20 St. Ambrose, On the Duties of Clergy, Book 3, Chapter 21:123, Nicene and Post-Nicene Fathers Series 2, Volume 10, Philip Schaff (ed.), p. 86

Mordecai, Esther was well pleasing to the king, and went in and sat instead of Vashti, who did not do his will; and because of Jesus, the Church is well pleasing to God, and has gone in to the king, instead of the congregation which did not His Will. Mordecai admonished Esther that she should fast with her maidens, that she and her people might be delivered from the hands of Haman; and Jesus admonished the Church and her children (to fast), that she and her children might be delivered from the wrath. Mordecai received the honor of Haman, his persecutor; and Jesus received great glory from His Father, instead of His persecutors who were of the foolish People. Mordecai trod upon the neck of Haman, his persecutor; and as for Jesus, His enemies shall be put under His feet. Before Mordecai, Haman proclaimed, Thus shall it be done to the man, in honoring whom the king is pleased; and as for Jesus, His preachers came out of the People that persecuted Him, and they said:—This is Jesus the Son of God. The blood of Mordecai was required at the hand of Haman and his sons; and the blood of Jesus, His persecutors took upon themselves and upon their children.[21]

What a beautiful passage that demonstrates the image of Christ in the pages of a book written well before His incarnation. This not only images Christ but illumines for us the various aspects of Christ's sacrifice and His call for us as members of the Church. There is much in this book that is very similar to the previous Book of Judith. Both women are unlikely defenders of their people—one is a widow and the other an orphan. Yet similar virtues enabled them to win victory over their adversaries. Also, the arrogant man who plots to become god and establish his will over all is doomed to fall. Esther provides much to contemplate and gives us courage to face evil in our own hearts, knowing that God will hear the humble of heart and deliver us from sin, death, and destruction.

---

21 St. Aphrahat, Select Demonstrations: On Persecution 21:20, Nicene and Post-Nicene Fathers Series 2, Volume 10, Philip Schaff (ed.), p. 400

## CHAPTER 6

1 Maccabees

The Septuagint contains three Books of the Maccabees. A fourth is often included as an appendix in many Orthodox copies of Scripture.

BACKGROUND AND SUMMARY

All the Maccabean books focus on themes of heroic resistance and martyrdom. The Books of the Maccabees take place from around 221 to 136 BC, which makes them an important transition from the time of the prophets till the coming of the Messiah. Historically, they set the stage for resistance against the great empires of Greece and Rome. Jewish nationalism begins to take root, and the desire for a restored monarchy that would lead Israel back into the glory of the Davidic Kingdom starts to grow. The name Maccabees comes from a heroic man in the books named Judas, given the surname Maccabeus, which means "the hammer" in Hebrew. His spirit of resistance and faithfulness to the covenant pervades all these books.

Structurally, this first book provides a setting for all the events that follow, beginning with the world conquest of Alexander the Great. After the historical introduction, the book divides into three sections, corresponding to the three leaders of the house of Maccabees. Mattathias, the father and patriarch of the family, begins his revolt in chapters 1 & 2. Judas, the son of Mattathias, from whom the name Maccabees is taken, leads the people in chapters 3 through 9:22. From there till the conclusion, Judas's brothers Jonathan and Simon lead and rule Israel.

The rise and conquest of Alexander and the establishment of the Greek Empire is the context of this whole period. Persia had been the ruling empire till this point in history. The events of Esther and Tobit took place in that Persian era. Now begins a new era for the Jews. Alexander's conquest covered much of the known world and aggressively spread the Greek language and culture. Emperors before him found other ways to unify their empires, but Alexander used the Greek language and ideas.

The spreading of a common language provided a means of trade and intellectual commerce as never before. This factor probably contributed to bringing about the "fullness of time" for the coming of Christ. For at no previous point in history (since the Tower of Babel, that is) could much of the world communicate in one tongue. Thus the Jews translated their Scripture into Greek. This translation became the Old Testament of the early Church. The apostles wrote their Gospels and epistles in Greek so the gospel could be spread beyond the parochial walls of Jerusalem. Greek remained a major language of commerce and education up till the fall of the Eastern Roman Empire in 1453 at the hands of the Ottoman Turks. This was Alexander's legacy.

Alexander died an untimely death at a young age, before a true perpetuation plan for the empire could be determined. After his death, his empire was divided up among his generals into five smaller kingdoms. At this point the story of the Maccabees begins.

One general took the area of Palestine, and his descendant, Antiochus Epiphanes, ruled over the area of Palestine and Judea. Antiochus was fanatical about hellenizing his subjected people, especially as it related to pagan religion. This created tension for the Jews. Many Jews abandoned their own religion to become pagan Greeks and recognize Antiochus as king. The apostate Jews received political power from Antiochus as a result. They built Greek stadiums, schools, and gymnasiums in Jerusalem and abandoned the practice of circumcising their male children.

The final straw for the faithful Jews was when Antiochus came to Jerusalem and entered the temple, taking all the sacred treasures. Then he sent an order "to forbid whole burnt offerings and sacrifices and drink offerings in the sanctuary, to profane the Sabbaths and the feasts, and to defile the sanctuary and the holy ones . . . to sacrifice swine and common animals" (1:45–47). The desecration of the temple was what filled the hearts of the people with sadness and shame. Many stood firm against Antiochus's reforms and faced martyrdom.

The brutality of the king was beyond comprehension. He put to death women who circumcised their sons into the covenant of Abraham. He killed the mothers and "hung the infants from their mothers' necks" (1:61). You can imagine the anger and rage that rose up in the hearts of many who remained faithful, and the despair caused by the attack and potential eradication of their faith.

In the midst of the people lived an excellent family. The patriarch was Mattathias from the tribe of Simeon. He was a priest with five sons: John, Simon, Judas, Eleazar, and Jonathan. He cried out one morning, "Alas, why was I born to see this, the ruin of my people, the destruction of the holy city" (2:7). Then he and his sons tore their clothes and mourned the fate of Jerusalem.

The spark of revolt came soon after. In the city of Modein, the king's men came to enforce the religious changes. Because of Mattathias's position in the community, he was asked first to follow the new decrees, yet he stridently refused to obey the king (2:19–21). Another Jewish man came forth from the crowd to sacrifice to the Greek idols; out of intense zeal, Mattathias ran forward and slew the man upon the pagan altar. After this, he and his children fled to the mountains. From there he became the leader of the resistance against Greek paganism. Many Jews followed him, and they eventually built up an army large enough to fight against Antiochus.

Eventually Mattathias and his followers expelled the Greeks, and under the leadership of Mattathias's son Judas, the land was liberated. Jerusalem was reclaimed and the temple restored. Judas then established an annual eight-day celebration for the rededication of the temple, referred to at the time of Christ as the Festival of Lights and known today as Hanukkah (4:52–59).

Judas continued to fight against successor after successor of Antiochus, and eventually made a treaty with the Roman Republic to come to the aid of Israel. This treaty with Rome and eventually with Sparta was reasserted by Judas's brothers Simon and Jonathan, who succeeded him. The remainder of the book describes various battles that continued to be waged to protect the land of Israel under the leadership of the sons of Mattathias.

WHAT WE CAN LEARN

The Church Fathers and early Christian writers see the courage and faith of the men of Maccabees and naturally apply it to Christians facing persecution and death under pagan Rome. Courage, the testing of faith, and the nature of persecution are major themes the Fathers find in 1 Maccabees. Tertullian explores an understanding of the Sabbath that even informs our understanding of Jesus' words on the Sabbath.

In chapter 2, at the beginning of the conflict with the Greeks under the leadership of Mattathias, the initial battles were fought in the wilderness outside of Modein. The Greeks and apostate Jews knew the followers of Mattathias were committed to upholding the covenant and used this against them. The battle was declared on the Sabbath, yet the resistance cried out, "We will not come out, nor will we do the will of the king to desecrate the Sabbath day" (2:34). The king's men rose up and slaughtered the defenseless men along with their women and children.

Mattathias grieved for them and resolved not to let their faith be destroyed by an overly strict adherence to the law. Love for their faith and heritage won out, and he declared, "Every man who comes against us for battle on the Sabbath day, let us war against him, and we shall not all die as our brothers did in their hiding places" (2:41).

It is this story on which the early Church theologian Tertullian comments, "For in the times of the Maccabees, too, they did bravely in fighting on the Sabbaths, and routed their foreign foes, and recalled the law of their fathers to the primitive style of life by fighting on the Sabbaths. Nor should I think it was any other law which they thus vindicated, than the one in which they remembered the existence of the prescript touching 'the day of the Sabbaths.'"[22]

Tertullian is pointing out that the need for the Maccabean fighters to defend their faith on the Sabbath is evidence of fluidity about the strictness of the Sabbath. Perhaps this passage in Maccabees is what Jesus is alluding to in Mark 2:27 when He says that the Sabbath was made for man and not man for the Sabbath. Love and mercy trump law.

It is the heroic resistance to evil and willingness to suffer and die for the faith that enchanted the Fathers with this book. Hippolytus, in his commentary on Daniel, refers to the lives of these Maccabean heroes as a fulfillment of Daniel's dream in Daniel 11.[23] Daniel speaks of the breakup of Alexander's empire and the struggles between the various Greek kings. Then Antiochus enters the scene, defiling the temple and creating a climate for Jewish revolt, and "the people who know their God will be strong and do valiantly" (Daniel 11:32). The Greek king will persecute the faithful, and "when they are weak, they shall be aided with a little help" (Daniel 11:34). According to Hippolytus, this refers to Mattathias and his son, because many were martyred who had cried out, "We will not come out, nor will we do the will of the king. . . . Let us all die in our innocence" (1 Maccabees 2:34, 37). This is the battle cry of the faithful in the face of external persecution or internal struggle. Death and despair may be victorious in this life, but the soul of the faithful will remain united to God eternally.

St. Ambrose, in Book 1, chapters 40 & 41 of his *On the Duties of Clergy,* writes of the virtues of the men of 1 Maccabees. These men are worthy of emulation because their hearts were steely and their faces set like flint against wickedness that sought to destroy their faith. Ambrose focuses on the faithful who were slaughtered at the beginning of the Maccabean conflict, Eleazar and Judas Maccabeus, and

---

22 Tertullian, An Answer to the Jews, Chapter 4, Ante-Nicene Fathers, Volume 3, Philip Schaff (ed.), p. 156

23 St. Hippolytus, On Daniel, Chapter 2:10, 11, Ante-Nicene Fathers, Volume 5, Philip Schaff (ed.), p. 180

gives three examples of their fortitude and faith. He begins, "First, I will speak of the people of our fathers. They were ready to fight for the temple of God." [24] These men took their faith seriously and were unwilling to be defiled at any cost. But they were willing to die so their family could practice their faith and worship God in peace.

The second example of fortitude and faith is the man Eleazar. The Greeks Antiochus V and Lysias began a campaign against Judas and his men. The Greeks brought elephants with them into battle and even intoxicated them with wine beforehand (6:34). Eleazar, one of Judas's warriors, saw an elephant dressed in royal armor and "reasoned the king was riding it." He rushed into the thick of the Greek phalanx, killing men on his left and right along the way. He slid under the elephant and sliced it from beneath. This brought down the beast, but Eleazar was crushed under its weight and "was buried in his own triumph."[25] Soon afterward, Antiochus asked for peace with the Jews.

Ambrose praises Eleazar, saying, "he left peace as the heir of his courage [and] these are the signs of triumph."[26] This was his legacy. The fearlessness and courage this man displayed in the face of certain death should embolden the hearts of all Christians called to fight against the wiles of the devil and against the wild beasts and hidden serpents that lurk in each man's heart. Each Christian must struggle to bring the Prince of Peace within his heart, "for the weapons of our warfare are not carnal but mighty in God for pulling down strongholds, casting down arguments and every high thing that exalts itself against the knowledge of God, bringing every thought into captivity to the obedience of Christ, and being ready to punish all disobedience when your obedience is fulfilled" (1 Corinthians 10:4–6).

St. Ambrose approaches the third example with the exhortation, "Fortitude is proved not only by prosperity but also in adversity; let us now consider the death of Judas Maccabeus."[27] After another

---

24   St. Ambrose, On the Duties of Clergy, Book 1, Chapter 40:206, Nicene and Post-Nicene Fathers Series 2, Volume 10, Philip Schaff (ed.), p. 33

25   Op. cit., 40:208, p. 34

26   Op. cit., 40:208, p. 34

27   Op. cit., 41:209, p. 34

general, Nicanor, was defeated, the Greek King Demetrius sent two more of his captains back into the land of Judah to squash the rebellion of Judas Maccabeus. Soon 20,000 troops were in place to engage Judas and his eight hundred men, a number that had just been lessened by deserting soldiers. Judas rallied the remaining men with an inspiring speech and attacked the Greek forces. Soon he discovered the Greek battle tactics, attacked their right flank, and routed them. But the Greek left flank discovered Judas's strategies and reversed course toward Judas. Judas fell, and his men fled.

It was not only Judas's courage in battle that uplifted Ambrose, but his final words. When his men wanted to surrender to the pagan forces, Judas cried out, "May it be far from us to do such a thing, to run away from them. If our time has come to die, then let us die courageously for the sake of our people. We will not leave behind a charge against our honor" (1 Maccabees 9:10). This should be another battle cry of the Church. No matter what the cost to ourselves, our glory is Christ, and we must live and fight so as not to sully His pure Body. Ambrose closes his comments on Judas with this encomium: "Thus he found the spot of death more full of glory for himself than any triumph."[28] May our lives be filled with such passion and courage for our Savior.

Let us finish with the comments of St. Cyprian of Carthage on 1 Maccabees. Cyprian takes two complementary ideas from this book. First he addresses the truth that trials in the life of a Christian are allowed by God so that the Christian might be proved. He then quotes Mattathias, as he exhorts his children to continue standing firm in the faith. Mattathias cites their great patriarch Abraham because "Abraham [was] found faithful in trial, and it was reckoned to him as righteousness" (1 Maccabees 2:52).

Secondly, Cyprian addresses another clergyman who is facing great trial and pressure by heretics. Courage is needed to bolster this man's resolve to be faithful and endure whatever the enemies of the faith may bring him. Again Cyprian quotes from Mattathias's final speech to his sons.

---

28   Op. cit., 41:209, p. 34

Mattathias has recalled all the great men of Israel from Abraham to Daniel. Each had his own trials, and each faced opposition and even certain death. Their strength came from their hope in the Lord. Mattathias looks on evildoers from an eternal perspective. St. Cyprian quotes him saying, "Do not fear the words of a sinful man, because his glory is like manure and worms. Today he will be exalted, but tomorrow he will not be found; for he returned to his dust, and his purpose will perish" (1 Maccabees 2:62, 63).[29] These words are strength in the face of the enemy. They provide a heavenly perspective and vindication for a life lived in faithfulness to the Lord.

The Book of 1 Maccabees provides encouragement and examples to fight the good fight and finish the race. It is not a promise of success or prosperity, or even of protection from evil in this life. It is an encouragement to all the faithful that there are those who have gone before us who were willing to sacrifice their lives and face the gates of hell with no certainty of the outcome. On this side of the resurrection, death is still real, but it has lost its stranglehold on mankind. The way of the cross is still a way of pain, yet the road is necessary, for it was trod by the One who has defeated death; it can take us through the dark night to the brightness of resurrection.

---

29 St. Cyprian, Epistles of St. Cyprian, 54:3, Ante-Nicene Fathers, Volume 5, Philip Schaff (ed.), p. 339

## CHAPTER 7

2 Maccabees

BACKGROUND AND SUMMARY

Whereas 1 Maccabees was concerned with the establishment of the Maccabean dynasty and their example of heroic faithfulness, 2 Maccabees focuses on correct theology, right belief, and right worship through the defense of Jerusalem.

The cast of characters one finds in 1 Maccabees populates this account as well. The focus of their struggles and the way the author arranges the text constitute the major differences between the two books. Some of the accounts have been expanded, and the book's structure makes it clear that the focus has shifted to Jerusalem and the defense of true belief and worship.

The author begins writing from Jerusalem to the Jews in Egypt about the events that have transpired in Jerusalem. At this point in history, a large population of Jews was living in Egypt. During the Babylonian captivity, many of the Jews remaining in Jerusalem who had not been taken as exiles into Babylon had emigrated to Egypt. It was out of this group that the translation of the Septuagint arose. Because Jerusalem was home for all Jews regardless of where they had been dispersed, news from the Holy City was always welcome.

The siege of Jerusalem, the retaking of the temple, and its rededication are retold; and the Egyptian Jews are encouraged to celebrate the feast of temple rededication, or Hanukkah. The story of the miracle of the altar fire under Nehemiah is retold, along with an account of the prophet Jeremiah carrying away into Egypt many of the sacred vessels of the temple to safeguard them for a time of restoration on that future date when the temple would be rebuilt. After this initial summary, the author slows the narrative and mentions the celebration of the purification of the temple. He collects his thoughts as he begins to summarize all the battles and intrigues under the Maccabees that led to the retaking of the temple of Jerusalem.

The story begins during the reign of the Greek king Seleucus IV (187–175 BC), when the Jews were favored and gifts were given to the temple. The godly Onias was the Jewish high priest at the time, but a certain man named Simon had become his enemy and tried to turn Seleucus's government against Onias. This traitor exaggerated the wealth of the temple to the Greek generals. This piqued their interest and led Seleucus to order Onias to give up the temple's treasure. The general Heliodorus was sent to Jerusalem to take the treasure from Onias, but Onias refused, saying the treasury was intended for orphans and widows. News of this crisis leaked into the streets of Jerusalem, and the people responded with fervent prayer.

God heard their prayers. Heliodorus approached the treasury, but "the Lord of spirits and all authority was already present" (2 Maccabees 3:24). Those accompanying Heliodorus were so afraid at this manifestation of God's power that they fled in terror. A horse and rider bedecked with full armor rushed upon him, striking him with the horse's front hooves. Two other strong young men appeared in glorious and noble apparel and struck the general blow upon blow.

Heliodorus fell and grew ill to the point of death, but Onias the high priest called upon the Lord for his healing. As Onias prayed, the angelic men appeared once more and said to Heliodorus, "'Be very grateful to Onias the high priest, for on his account the Lord has granted you your life. Now since you were punished by heaven, report to all men the majestic power of God'" (3:33, 34). Then they vanished. Heliodorus made sacrifices to the God of heaven and bore testimony to all his men of the power of God. The temple treasury was saved.

After Seleucus died and Antiochus Epiphanes became king, Onias was dethroned and banished by his deceptive brother, Jason, and Jason was given the office of high priest. Jason made many concessions to the Greeks and began a program of Hellenization that included offering money for sacrifice to the Greek pantheon. Jason is a Greek name, not a Hebrew one, and one wonders whether Jason took this name as part of a Greek identity.

A more corrupt Jew named Menelaus (also a Greek name) bribed the generals and became high priest. Jason was driven out as a fugitive into the land of the Ammonites. During his reign, Menelaus used the temple treasury to bribe the various Greek officials. The former high priest Onias discovered his actions and publicly condemned him. In retaliation, Menelaus had one of his officials, Andronicus, murder Onias. Both Jews and Greeks were outraged at this senseless killing. Even the pagan Antiochus Epiphanes felt sorrow and executed Andronicus. However, Menelaus continued his evil ways during his time as high priest.

Antiochus Epiphanes planned another attack on Egypt, leaving Jerusalem for his military campaign. A rumor spread that Antiochus was dead. The former evil high priest, Jason, came back to Jerusalem with an army of one thousand and took a portion of the city. Jason was driven back and had to return to the Ammonites. Eventually he was banished from there, as well as from every place he tried to find refuge throughout his life. He died friendless, without family, and unmourned.

Antiochus heard of the Jerusalem uprising and left Egypt because he thought Judea was in revolt. He entered Jerusalem in a fury, killing every man, woman, and child in his march toward the temple. Menelaus, the high priest, brought him in and showed him the temple treasury. Antiochus plundered the temple, oppressed the people, and even killed his Jewish opponents on the Sabbath (see 1 Maccabees). These actions of Antiochus sparked the beginnings of the Maccabean revolt.

In contrast to the apostate priests is a story of martyrdom that is at the heart of 2 Maccabees. Antiochus accelerated his program toward paganism in Jerusalem. He renamed the temple for the Olympian Zeus. Thus the temple became like pagan temples throughout the ancient world, including not only sacrifices to idols, but debauchery and temple prostitutes as well. The Jews were forced to sacrifice to idols and abandoned religious practices such as keeping the Sabbath and circumcising their infants.

The author retells horrific stories of martyrdom for those who held fast to their faith. The acts are so horrible that he even feels the need to theologize and explain why God would allow such persecution of His people. He concludes that the Lord allows such things to happen to His people that they may repent of their sin; God does not deal thus with the Gentiles, for He allows them to "attain the completion of their sins, then punishes them" (6:14). In spite of what was happening, God never "withdraws His mercy from us . . . [and] does not abandon His own people" (6:16).

One man, Eleazar, an old and respected scribe, refuses to sacrifice and eat what has been offered to idols. As a result, he goes willingly to the rack and is killed. As he is dying, he defends his martyrdom and proudly says, "I am enduring terrible sufferings in my body from this beating, but in my soul I gladly suffer these things because I fear Him" (6:30).

Then the martyrdom of seven brothers and their mother is recounted. They have been arrested by the king and put through horrific tortures. The first brother is tortured and killed in front of his mother and other brothers. The second is then tortured and killed before them, and this continues until all the brothers are dead. The author praises this mother who watched the death of each of her children yet encouraged them in faithfulness to God: "Filled with a noble spirit, she stirred her womanly reasoning with manly courage" (7:21).

From chapter 8 onward, the book summarizes the campaigns of Judas Maccabeus against the Greeks, first under Antiochus Epiphanes, then under Antiochus IV, and finally under Demetrius. It is within this portion of the book that many aspects of the Church's theology are demonstrated.

The deaths of Antiochus Epiphanes and the evil high priest Menelaus are also recounted. Antiochus continued in his arrogance with a plan to exterminate the Jews. God struck him with affliction and pain in his "inward parts." He fell from his chariot and his body was racked with more pain. Then "worms swarmed up from the ungodly man's body, and his flesh rotted away while he was still alive" (9:9). The smell from his body was so horrible that few would attend to him. Eventually he offered remorse to God, but died in a foreign land after designating his son Antiochus V to take his place.

Menelaus died with dishonor as well. Under the reign of Antiochus V, he attempted to bargain and support the king against his own people. The king and his guardian recognized that Menelaus was a treacherous man and threw him from a high tower. He was crushed at its base in a pit of ashes. He was deprived of burial, and the author says this was justice because "since he committed many sins against the sacred altar, whose fire and ashes were holy, he should get death for himself in ashes" (13:8).

The author helps the reader to see the purpose behind the retelling of these events. He inserts his own editorial comments in many places, reminding the reader of the importance of right belief and right worship. Jerusalem and the worship in the temple are central to the purpose of this book. This provides a nice contrast to 1 Maccabees, which tells many similar stories but focuses more on the heroism of faithfulness and the establishment of the Maccabean dynasty. In this book, the Maccabees are but stewards who usher in a time of restored faith and worship.

THE NEW TESTAMENT & THEOLOGY

One of the biggest influences 2 Maccabees has had on further scripture and theology is on martyrology. The story of Eleazar, the seven brothers, and their mother provides the kernel for understanding and embracing martyrdom. This was especially important in the early Church, because from Pentecost to the conversion of Constantine, Christians were in constant danger of torture and death. It was this period that established forever a sense of hope and sacrifice in the face of certain death.

Throughout the Gospels, Jesus promises that those who follow Him will suffer and experience persecution. The life of Christ reveals the way of the cross as the way to resurrection, and illuminates that which was understood in 2 Maccabees as but a shadow. The

Maccabean martyrs saw their martyrdom as an offering of worship or sacrifice to the Most High. This is ultimately fulfilled in Christ, who is the perfect sacrifice offered to God. The sacrifices of the Maccabees and of all Christians share in the sacrifice of Christ. St. Paul expands on this theme by calling Christians to be "a living sacrifice" (Romans 12:1). For if you are never a living sacrifice, then you may not be able to make the ultimate sacrifice if called on to do so in this life.

In 2 Maccabees, the martyred mother anticipates humanity's resurrection gained through the death and Resurrection of Jesus. She cries out to one of her children before their death, "Therefore the Creator of the world, who formed man in the beginning and devised the origin of all things, will give both breath and life back to you again in His mercy" (7:23). For the hope of resurrection destroys the fear of death and brings power to stand strong in the face of death. Her final words sum up this hope for all who face the powers of death in this life: "Do not fear this executioner! But be worthy of your brothers and accept death, that in God's mercy I may receive you back again with your brothers" (7:29).

These martyrs are unique, and even though they are Old Testament saints prior to the life of Christ, they are memorialized in the Church's commemoration of saints. In the hymns they are referred to as Christ's holy martyrs interceding for the world. They are celebrated in the Church on August 1/14. Here are the troparion and kontakion for the feast respectively:

Let us praise the seven Maccabees, with their mother Salome and their teacher Eleazar; they were splendid in lawful contest as guardians of the teachings of the Law. Now as Christ's holy martyrs they ceaselessly intercede for the world.

Seven pillars of the Wisdom of God and seven lampstands of the divine Light, all-wise Maccabees, greatest of the martyrs before the time of the martyrs, with them ask the God of all to save those who honor you.

Another significant passage is found in chapter 12 during one of Judas's campaigns against the Greeks. After one battle, the evening of Sabbath was drawing near, so Judas and his men left the field, purified themselves according to the law, and celebrated the Sabbath. The next day, they went back to retrieve the bodies of their fallen comrades in order to give them a proper burial. Under the cloaks of these men they discovered tokens of pagan idolatry. Shocked, they immediately prayed for these dead men that "the sin they had committed might be completely blotted out" (12:42). They not only prayed for the souls of these men, but took up an offering and sent it to Jerusalem to be presented as a sin offering.

The author comments that had Judas not been looking for the resurrection, it would have been foolish to pray for these dead men. "But since [Judas] was looking to the reward of splendor laid up for those who repose in godliness, it was a holy and godly purpose. Thus he made atonement for the fallen, so as to set them free from their transgression" (12:45). This passage is evidence that the Jews offered prayers for their departed. This practice was present during the time of Christ and was continued by the early Church. For the Church, however, unlike the Maccabean Jews, the resurrection was no mere speculation but reality because of the revelation of Jesus Christ.

A final passage to mention is from chapter 15. This is a wonderful passage that demonstrates the intercession of the saints for those struggling on earth.

During his reign, the Greek king Demetrius chose a man named Nicanor as governor of Judea. On one occasion, Nicanor had learned that Judas and his men were in Samaria, and Nicanor planned to attack them on the Sabbath. The Jews in Nicanor's contingent persuaded him not to defile the Sabbath. Instead, Nicanor arrogantly erected a monument proclaiming his victory over Judas and his army before any battle had been fought.

Judas's army was demoralized as a result and had a sense of impending defeat. Judas gathered the troops to encourage them to trust in the Lord because God had protected them in times past and given victory. In order to inspire his men, he told them a vision he had seen.

In this vision, Judas sees Onias, the deceased godly high priest, praying with hands outstretched for the whole nation of the Jews. Praying with Onias is a gray-headed man having a "certain astonishing and majestic preeminence" (15:13). Onias identifies this man as the prophet Jeremiah, who loves his people and prays fervently for them. Onias at this time was recently departed, yet Jeremiah had been dead for over three hundred years. Jeremiah gives Judas a golden sword and tells him that it is from God to strike down his enemies.

This vision rallied the men and they entered the battle against Nicanor with invocations and prayers. They won the battle and found Nicanor's body while they were returning home from the battle. The vision of their departed saints interceding for them was understood as a visitation by God, and "they fought with their hands and prayed to God in their hearts" (15:27). This story affirms the Jews' belief in the intercession of the saints. The Church continues to ask for help from the saints, who love us and pray fervently for us in the battlefield of life.

Not only does the Church find doctrinal virtue in this book, it has also become source material for hymnology. The hymn for the Maccabean martyrs was quoted above, but the Church also uses the victory over the evil general Heliodorus for song. The warrior armored in gold sitting on a powerful horse that attacked Heliodorus as he attempted to enter the temple is identified as the Archangel Michael. This account is retold in Ikos 9 of the Akathist to St. Michael:

Hail, unconquerable leader of the armies of Orthodoxy!
Hail, very fear and defeat of armies whose beliefs are evil!
Hail, planter of the Orthodox faith and worship!
Hail, uprooter of heresies and schisms that harm the soul!
Hail, you who strengthened the pious Maccabees on the
    field of battle!
Hail, you who struck down in the temple itself Heliodorus,
    the captain of the evil king, Antiochus!

Hail, Michael, great chief captain with all the hosts of
> heaven!

These nuggets of spiritual counsel are but a sample of the riches
that can be mined out of a book that appears to be a mere historical
record.

WISDOM FROM THE FATHERS

The repeated examples of martyrdom throughout 2 Maccabees provided inspiration to the embattled early Church. St. Cyprian's *Exhortation to Martyrdom Addressed to Fortunatus* quotes frequently from
this book. The academic Origen also penned an *Exhortation to Martyrdom,* in which he referred to the story of the seven brothers and
their fearless mother. Of the seven brothers St. Ambrose says:

> The company of the seven brothers stood unconquered
> though surrounded by the legions of the king—tortures
> failed, tormentors ceased; but the martyrs failed not. One,
> having had the skin of his head pulled off, though changed
> in appearance, grew in courage. Another, bidden to put forth
> his tongue, so that it might be cut off . . . What shall I say of
> the mother who with joy looked on the corpses of her chil-
> dren as so many trophies, and found delight in the voices of
> her dying sons, as though in the songs of singers, noting in
> her children the tones of the glorious harp of her own heart,
> and a sweeter harmony of love than any strain of the lute
> could give?[30]

St. Basil, in a letter to a Christian woman who has just lost her
son and is experiencing great trials, compares the martyrdom of
the Maccabean children to her own suffering.[31] Although she is not

---

30 St. Ambrose, On the Duties of Clergy, Book 1, Chapter 41:211, Nicene and
    Post-Nicene Fathers Series 2, Volume 10, Philip Schaff (ed.), p. 34
31 St. Basil the Great, The Letters: 6, To the Wife of Nectarius, Nicene and Post-
    Nicene Fathers Series 2, Volume 8, Philip Schaff (ed.), p. 115

experiencing literal martyrdom, this trial provides similar spiritual benefits.

Early in 2 Maccabees we read the story of the miraculous hidden fire that provides the basis for the Jewish feast of Hanukkah. St. Ephrem (along with Clement of Alexandria), in his Epiphany hymns, sees this story as a type of the Holy Spirit hidden within each Christian:

> The captive priests again in the well
> hid and concealed the fire of the sanctuary,
> a mystery of that glorified fire
> which the High Priest mingles in Baptism.
> The priests took up of the mire,
> and on the altar they sprinkled it;
> for its fire, the *fire* of that well,
> with the mire had been mingled;
> a mystery of our bodies which in the water
> with the fire of the Holy Spirit have been mingled.[32]

For in receiving the Holy Spirit at baptism, we take the fire of God into our being. This fire can transform us into the likeness of God or condemn us. The fire should be held in fear and reverence as we submit ourselves to its working in our lives.

St. Ambrose also admires the example of the high priest Onias. No matter the pressure he faced from his people and enemies, he was a faithful steward of all that God had entrusted to him.[33] He used the temple treasury to help the poor and weak and not to enrich his own pockets.

Finally, St. Hilary of Poitiers points out the assertion that God made the world out of nothing.[34] This was asserted by the martyred

---

32 St. Ephrem the Syrian, Hymns for the Feast of the Epiphany: Hymn 8, Nicene and Post-Nicene Fathers Series 2, Volume 13, Philip Schaff (ed.), p. 277

33 St. Ambrose, On the Duties of Clergy, Book 2, Chapter 29, Nicene and Post-Nicene Fathers Series 2, Volume 10, Philip Schaff (ed.), p. 65, 66

34 St. Hilary of Poitiers, On the Trinity: Book 4, Nicene and Post-Nicene Fathers Series 2, Volume 9, Philip Schaff (ed.), p. 73

mother in her speech to her sons before the king. This is a doctrine that has been held by all Christians, Orthodox, Catholic, and Protestant, yet it is only explicitly stated in the books of the Readables, which are rejected by Protestants. To come to a similar conclusion, Protestant scholars must make logical progressions from other statements in Scripture.

The Book of 2 Maccabees is full of truth about God and man, and it contains the seeds of Christian revelation. It is no wonder the early Church and the Fathers embraced this book as their own.

## CHAPTER 8

# 3 Maccabees

BACKGROUND & SUMMARY

This book has no real relation to events found in the other two Books of Maccabees. However, it describes a similar resistance of the Jews in Egypt just prior to the Maccabean period, and in this resistance it is Maccabean in spirit.

In Egypt, the Greek dynasty was known as the Ptolemaic dynasty, and the ruler in this account was Philopater, also known as Ptolemy IV. The Greek ruler in Palestine at this time was Antiochus III, the father of Antiochus (IV) Epiphanes, whom we have seen in the other Maccabean books. The Greek empire after Alexander the Great was not a united front, but composed of Greek kingdoms fighting each other for dominance.

Philopater attacked the forces of Antiochus around the city of Gaza and prevailed. Because of his success, he planned a tour of the local area to garner support for himself and the Ptolemaic dynasty as against the dynasty of Antiochus. He learned of the temple in Jerusalem and desired to go there to see and perhaps worship. While there, he made appropriate offerings, but then wanted to enter the inner portion of the temple. The Jews refused and explained that even the high priest was only allowed to go in once a year. The king insisted. The priests cried out to God to prevent the desecration. The Jewish people heard the cries of the priests, and a near riot erupted in the streets with protests. The king's counselors, seeing the protests, encouraged the king not to enter the temple, but he insisted.

Simon, the high priest, knelt and said a fervent prayer to God. In his prayer, he first offers praise to God, then recounts various times that God delivered His people from arrogant men. He includes the men of Sodom, the Egyptian Pharaoh, and the Philistine giants as examples of strong men God overthrew. Jerusalem is praised as the center of true worship and the heart of Israel. Because of this, Simon asks that God protect the temple, forgive the people's sins, and show compassion on them.

The prayers were heard, and Ptolemy did not enter the temple because he began to tremble so violently he could not stand. His bodyguards dragged him away and carried him back to Egypt. Unfortunately, when he recovered, Ptolemy still did not repent but continued his threats against Israel.

This event turned Ptolemy against the Jews, and his anger was directed against the Jews in Egypt. He required that a census of all Egyptian Jews be taken and that they be made slaves. They were branded with an ivy leaf, symbol of the Greek god Dionysius, reminding modern readers of the marks the Nazis used to distinguish the Jews. If the Jews refused, they were killed; but some could escape if they embraced paganism. Unfortunately, some Jews apostatized, and the comments regarding them are sobering and challenging to all who commit their lives to Christ: "Some, then, obviously hated the price required to maintain godliness in the city. So they gave themselves up willingly, for they expected greater glory from the association they were about to have with the king" (2:31). Thankfully, most held fast and often found other ways to avoid slavery.

Because so many found loopholes in the law and avoided slavery, Ptolemy was filled with rage at the Jews. False witness was spread against the Jews, and many Gentiles began to hate and fear them. There were some among the Greeks who took notice of their righteous behavior and tried to protect them from the state.

Ptolemy sent out a decree and ordered all the Jews in Egypt to be arrested and brought to the coliseum in Alexandria. He ordered his soldiers to gather five hundred elephants and intoxicate them with wine. The elephants were to be released into the throng of Jews and trample them to death for all to witness.

The Jews offered prayers for protection to God, and the king fell into a deep sleep which postponed their demise. When he awoke, he was enraged that he had missed the opportunity of daylight to destroy his newly hated people. He promised that in the morning of the next day, he would execute his plan.

At dawn he gathered the entire city as spectators to this awful genocide. The Jews again raised their hands in prayer, and when the time to release the beasts came, Ptolemy could not remember his commands. The people were delivered once again. During the evening banquet, Ptolemy again summoned the elephant keeper and instructed him regarding the Jews' destruction in the coliseum the following day.

This time it appeared the Jews would not escape, for they could see the dust kicked up by the elephants coming through the gates. Eleazar, an elderly Jewish priest, gathered the elders around himself and called on God in prayer. In his prayer, he mentioned Daniel, the Three Holy Youths, and Jonah. Two angels descended from heaven, striking fear in the hearts of everyone but the Jews. The angels attacked the enemy forces, the king was mute with terror, and the drunken elephants turned on the soldiers.

The king's heart began to change, and he acted as if he had never initiated these events. He freed the Jews that were enslaved and sent the others home. He even held a week-long feast for the Jews. Ptolemy sent out a letter to his kingdom pardoning the Jews and extolling the virtues of their religion. The Jews left in peace and were even given permission to punish those of their religion who had apostatized.

USE IN THE CHURCH

The Fathers have little to say about this book. Unlike 2 Maccabees, which seemed filled with illustrations and theological nuggets that could be used to teach and defend Orthodoxy, this book is a simple example of God's deliverance of His people when they feared eradication. The prayer of Eleazar, the elderly priest, in chapter 6 provides a wonderful meditation on God's mercy and its ultimate fulfillment in the Resurrection of Jesus Christ.

Eleazar's prayer is one of desperation. He cries out to God, and drawing on the deep well of Scripture contained in his soul, he combines the themes of the Old Testament into a cry for mercy. The word "mercy" itself comes from a root meaning "olive oil," which was used to soothe and heal and even to anoint someone with God's power. At its core, mercy has a sense of healing and restoration, not necessarily a legal release from punishment. This is man's ultimate need, and when pressed to desperation it can be man's ultimate cry.

A short search on the word "mercy" in the Gospels reveals that it is primarily used as a petition by those in deep need. They are calling out to Jesus to "have mercy" on their soul. Not only is this man's ultimate need, but it is God's ultimate act. Every action of God toward mankind is one of mercy, from creation to redemption. As Orthodox believers, we cry "Lord have mercy" or "Lord Jesus Christ Son of God, have mercy on me a sinner" multiple times throughout our services and daily lives. We pray thus because we need God's mercy on every aspect of our lives, and because we need to believe and be convinced in our own hearts that God has mercy. He is a good God and loves mankind, and He is constantly pouring out His healing and restorative mercy upon us. We have difficulty believing this, so we must pray for it always to remind ourselves of God's eternal action toward us.

Eleazar begins by describing God as one who "governs all creation in mercy" (6:2). He concludes his prayer by asking for mercy (6:12) and quotes from Leviticus 26:44, which describes God's promise of deliverance if the people's sin leads them to destruction. Regardless of the state of sin and oppression Israel falls into, God will not let them be utterly destroyed because when "they were in the land of their enemies, [God] did not neglect them nor treat them with contempt" (Leviticus 26:44). Mercy covers all.

In the midst of these pleas for mercy, Eleazar recites events of history in which God poured out mercy in hopeless situations. God delivered Israel from an arrogant Pharaoh in the Exodus from Egypt, and He protected Jerusalem from destruction by the Assyrian tyrant Sennacherib. When the Three Holy Youths were thrown into the fiery furnace and Daniel into the lions' den, God delivered them all. Even

Jonah, "decomposing in the belly of the deep-sea monster" (6:8), was returned unharmed to his family.

Each of these examples is an image of the ultimate act of mercy—Christ's crucifixion and glorious Resurrection, freeing man from the power of the devil and trampling down death by death. The Pharaoh is Satan, who is chasing man to keep him in bondage, but Christ destroys him in the "light of His mercy." Sennacherib, like Pharaoh, images the devil seeking to destroy the people of God, but Christ shatters him, making His "power visible to many nations." The fire of the Godhead at once saves the Holy Youths and destroys the enemy. Daniel is rescued from the gravelike den "back up to the daylight." And Jonah, truly buried and decomposing in the sea, is returned "unharmed to his kin." Each of these is a picture of the journey from the darkness of the grave to the light and fire of the resurrection.

Even in simple stories that seem nothing more than exciting tales of deliverance, Christ can be seen. The Old Testament is full of these accounts and images, just as Eleazar recounts in his prayer. Reading through the eyes of the cross, these stories are transformed from mere historical marvels to stories of eternal spiritual consequence.

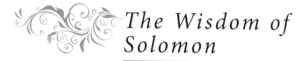 The Wisdom of Solomon

The previous books we have examined have been primarily historical texts that show God's hand working in the midst of events and the response of His people to God's actions. The next two books we will consider fit within the wisdom genre of Scripture. Other more familiar books that belong to this genre are the Books of Proverbs and Ecclesiastes.

Wisdom literature is characterized by short pithy statements of practical wisdom, praises of wisdom, the personification of wisdom, and comparisons and contrasts between the wise and the fool. In fact, wisdom is not mere learning, but the application of experience and the law of God in everyday life. Teachers in the wisdom tradition have observed the world through the lens of God's law and gleaned guidelines that improve man's relationship with the world around him without compromising his fidelity to the law of God. Those who are able to align their life to God's law are called wise, and those who cannot or will not are considered fools. It is not enough to merely know the law; wisdom comes from accurately applying it throughout the maze of life.

The Wisdom of Solomon may have been the last book in the Old Testament to be written. Its name does not denote authorship, but implies that the content of the book is a summary of the Solomonic wisdom tradition. God spoke to Solomon and offered him his heart's desire, and Solomon chose wisdom. He collected and shared much of this wisdom in the Books of Proverbs and Ecclesiastes. This book feels very similar to those works and is a clear continuation of the wisdom tradition. It is often referred to simply as "Wisdom" rather than by its full title.

One thing to remember in reading this book and all Old Testament wisdom literature books is that whenever Wisdom is personified, the Church always interprets this as referring to Jesus. Upon the revelation of Jesus Christ, wisdom as mere practical advice deepens. Wisdom is personal, and it is through the personal encounter with Wisdom that one is transformed into the image of God. Christ is the Wisdom of the Father, and this is evident in how the Church uses these texts.

STRUCTURE & SUMMARY

From the first few verses, the purpose and audience of the book are made known. It is written to rulers and kings and those "who judge the earth" (1:1). Then later, in chapter 6, the author again calls the mighty to listen and understand the wisdom of God. Earlier wisdom literature was often addressed to kings and rulers because Solomon was addressing his children and future kings; but at the time of this writing there was no king in Israel. Rulers existed, as we have read in Maccabees, but no kings proper such as under the Davidic monarchy.

So to whom would this book be applicable for instruction? Each town, community, family, and synagogue would have had rulers who led and made decisions. Ultimately, though, all men and women, especially those within the covenant of God's people, are rulers and kings. Each person is responsible for his own kingdom over which he must act as steward. This responsibility, no matter how small, requires wisdom and insight that should flow out of God's commandments. For this reason, all who read this book can learn and profit from this distillation of wisdom teaching.

The purpose of this book, then, is a defense of faith in the one true God and the value of wisdom that flows from Him. If we assume that the book was composed during the Maccabean period, this purpose becomes essential to the survival of the Jewish faith. Jews were being seduced into elaborate systems of Greek philosophy and the mysteries of pagan rites and rituals. Many apostatized into Greek ways, and those unwilling to leave the faith of their fathers lived under the threat of persecution and martyrdom.

The Wisdom of Solomon provides a sturdy framework of defense against both foreign philosophy and pagan idolatry. Encouragement to remain faithful and wisdom to navigate the narrow straits of an uncertain life are emphasized. These characteristics should make it evident why the early Church Fathers loved this work, and why it finds its way into the Church's liturgy.

The book divides easily into three major sections. The first section, chapters 1–5, demonstrates that God bestows eternal life and wisdom on man. It is from this section that the liturgical readings of the Church are taken. The second section, chapters 6–9, is a discussion of the nature and power of wisdom and King Solomon's pursuit of it. Solomon's pursuit should spur all the faithful to follow his example. Finally, in chapters 10–19, wisdom is seen at work throughout history, guiding the faithful through the trials and tribulations that arose in their own uncertain times. Again, guidance and encouragement through adherence to wisdom is paramount.

Let us look at each section in more detail, along with the key passage that summarizes its content.

Chapters 1–5 proclaim that eternal life and wisdom come from God. The author begins by setting up a contrast between the one who seeks righteousness and wisdom and the one who rejects them. This contrast remains constant throughout this section. The choice made by the sinner and the righteous is ultimately between life and death, which becomes clear at the end of chapter 1. God did not create death and takes no pleasure in the death of man, but a life of ungodliness makes a pact with death that leads to destruction. From this point, the responses and reactions of the wicked man alternate with those of the righteous. The wicked see death as inescapable and descend into a life of sensuality; the righteous hold fast to God and escape death. The key passage of this section is 3:1–9:

> But the souls of the righteous are in the hand of God,
> And no torture will ever touch them.

In the eyes of the undiscerning they seemed to have died,
And their departure was considered to be misfortune,
And their passage from us to be their destruction;
But they are at peace.
For though in man's view they were punished,
Their hope is full of immortality.
Though chastened in a few things,
Great kindness will be shown them,
For God tested them and found them worthy of Himself.
He tested them like gold in a furnace
And accepted them as a whole burnt offering.
In the time of their visitation they will shine forth,
And they will run about like sparks through straw.
They will judge nations and rule over peoples,
And the Lord shall reign over them unto the ages.
Those who trust in Him will understand truth,
And the faithful shall continue with Him in love,
Because grace and mercy are upon His elect.

Within this passage the heart of the righteous is on display. The world sees the fate of the righteous from one perspective, but through the eyes of God and those who partake of His wisdom, the true destiny of the righteous is clear. Torture and persecution may come upon the godly, but "it will never touch them." The righteous will not be delivered from the physical pain of suffering they may endure, but it will have no effect on their soul.

A Jew reading this could hearken back to the recent story of the Maccabean martyrs and recognize that the horrors they suffered did not affect their faith in God. They held fast, and their souls were not damaged by torture. However, they did not remain untouched. They were changed, but not in a way the world would understand. Their death was an act of worship and love because they remained faithful to their God. Just as gold in a furnace is purified, these righteous ones were as well, and now they shine in holiness reflecting the likeness of their Creator.

The early Church would have identified with this passage in that eternal life flows from Christ the Lord. Just like these Old Testament martyrs, they too would undergo horrible persecution under the Roman yoke. They could proclaim that their martyrs now shone through the heavens and were reigning with Christ in heaven. As St. Gregory the Theologian says, "Light is also the brilliancy of heaven to those who have been purified here, when the righteous shall shine forth as the Sun, and God shall stand in the midst of them, gods and kings, deciding and distinguishing the ranks of the Blessedness of heaven."[35]

These martyrs became the Church's intercessors for those remaining in the earthly arena as they continued to do battle with the forces of darkness. Ultimately, this passage speaks of Christ Himself, for He offered the only complete whole burnt offering of Himself to the Father. No torture ever touched Him, and the gold of His divinity was manifest through the Cross and subsequent Resurrection. It is only through uniting with Christ in the Cross that what is spoken of in this passage becomes true for mankind.

The Church uses this passage during Vespers for the Sunday of All Saints because it describes a behind-the-scenes look at what happens in the life of all saints. Whether through martyrdom forced by an external enemy or spiritual martyrdom embraced through a life of asceticism, each saint is put through fire and comes forth shining like gold. Each saint is held in the palm of God, where "torture will not touch them" because their soul has been committed and united with Christ, their Lord. This passage becomes not only an explanation of the life of the godly, but an exhortation to embrace faith in Christ because eternal life flows from His hands.

The middle section of the book (chs. 6–9) is a description of the nature and power of Wisdom as well as King Solomon's pursuit of her. Once again kings and rulers are addressed and are upbraided for not ruling God's kingdom by God's counsel. Exhortation is given that will enable those ruling to conform their decisions to the wisdom

---

35 St. Gregory the Theologian, Oration 40: On Holy Baptism, Nicene and Post-Nicene Fathers Series 2, Volume 10, Philip Schaff (ed.), p. 361

of God. Wisdom is praised in such a way as to create a desire in the heart of the reader and to set the affections aright to pursue it with one's whole being.

An unnamed man appears on the scene describing his own pursuit of wisdom. Based on the account, King Solomon is the man in question. He describes his request for wisdom over power and riches, yet when it came to him the other things followed. This matches closely the accounts of Solomon found in the Book of 3 Kingdoms. In telling of his own pursuit, he reveals the nature of wisdom and how it works and manifests itself in life. Solomon ends this section in prayer to God, praising Him for wisdom. From this prayer comes a key passage that summarizes much of what this section has to say about wisdom.

> O God of our fathers and the Lord of mercy,
> Who made all things by Your word
> And in Your wisdom built a man,
> That by You He might be the master of what is created,
> And manage the world in holiness and righteousness,
> And pass judgment with uprightness of soul:
> Give me the wisdom that sits by Your throne,
> And do not reject me from among Your servants;
> Because I am Your servant and the son of Your
>   maidservant,
> A weak man and lasting but a short time,
> And inferior in the understanding of judgment and laws.
> For though one is perfect among the sons of men,
> Yet if Your wisdom is absent from him,
> He will be regarded as nothing. (9:1–6)

This teaches that God created man through wisdom. As Christians, we understand this to be the hand of Christ, and the New Testament will affirm Christ as the Creator. Man was created in order to have dominion over creation. Yet this dominion is not that of totalitarian cruelty, nor is it driven by human passions; it is stewardship according to equity, righteousness, and an upright heart. This dominion must be understood in the context of the command to be fruitful and multiply in order to spread the image of God throughout creation. Dominion must be aligned with the wisdom of God; otherwise, man's activities will be regarded as nothing. If the benchmark for dominion is Christ (for He is the Image) and Him crucified, then a radical picture of leadership and kingship emerges.

Wisdom throughout the history of God's people is the subject of the final section of the book. The section begins with wisdom creating Adam and imbuing him with the power to rule all things. Then the descent into sin begins, of which the first evidence is the murder of Abel by Cain. The destruction of the Flood, Sodom & Gomorrah, Abraham, Jacob, Joseph, Moses, and the wandering in the wilderness are presented from the perspective of wisdom. The guiding hand of wisdom moves through history and protects God's people, instructing and correcting man toward communion with God.

The reader is expected to know and understand each of the events and be intimately familiar with the Torah, for the people discussed are never named. Their stories are told, and their identities become apparent through knowledge of the early history of Israel. This again should demonstrate that the Wisdom tradition in Israel is merely a commentary and application of the Torah.

A clear example of this "anonymous" retelling is the Jacob section (10:10–12). Verse 10 says, "[Wisdom] guided a righteous man on straight paths / When he fled from his brother's wrath." This is a reference to Jacob's fleeing from the face of Esau. In the Noah section, there is a beautifully veiled prophecy or foreshadowing of the cross. For the Fathers, the story of the ark is often a type of the Church sailing through the waters of baptism and escaping the destruction of sin. In this passage, wisdom piloted the righteous man by a cheap piece of wood. It is through an unassuming structure of wood that Wisdom Himself, the true Righteous Man, defeated sin and death and brought life to mankind.

From this historical retelling, the author settles in on the contrast between Israel and Egypt. Within the pages of the Bible, Egypt becomes the symbol and placeholder for all things opposed to God. Its history in the Torah and interaction with Moses should be a clear reason it is used this way. Egypt is also an expression of the idolatry of mankind. Even when the people of Israel, under the leadership of Aaron, construct the golden calf for worship, they are seen as return-ing to Egypt. A contrast is drawn between Israel and Egypt in much the same way as other wisdom literature contrasts the wise man and the fool. This contrast centers primarily on the worship of the true God and the worship of idols.

Let us look at two key passages in this section that demonstrate this contrast and what it can teach regarding wisdom. Here is the first of these passages:

> For great power is always present with You,
> And who can oppose the might of Your arm?
> Because the entire world before You
> Is like a small additional weight on scales,
> And like a drop of dew early in the morning
> That falls on the ground.
> But You are merciful to all, for You can do all things;
> And You overlook the sins of men to bring them to
>   repentance.
> For You love all the things that exist,
> And You detest nothing of the things You made;
> For You would not even make anything You hated.
> How could anything continue to exist unless You willed it?
> Or how could anything be preserved
> Unless it was called into existence by You?
> You spare all things, because they are Yours,
> O Master who love human beings.
> For Your immortal Spirit is in all things.
> For this reason You correct little by little those who fall away,
> And You remind and warn them of the sins they commit
> So they may be freed from evil and believe in You, O Lord.
>   (11:21—12:2)

This passage follows the author's historical review, ending with Israel in the wilderness. In spite of all the Israelites' failings in their wanderings, wisdom was nearby, prodding and protecting. Even in the midst of open rebellion and sin, wisdom did not forsake the people, but led them ever on, even if slowly, toward a life of communion with God. The verses above summarize this never-failing love that wisdom has for the people of God. Once more, we see a glimpse of revelation that Wisdom is not some immaterial force in the mind of God, but a Person. This Old Testament revelation is fulfilled in the revelation of the Incarnation and eventually leads the Apostles and Fathers to connect Wisdom with the Person of Jesus Christ.

Wisdom is more powerful than anything humans can imagine, yet unlike a tyrannical ruler outraged at the horrific sins of men, Wisdom has mercy. Wisdom is the Creator and loves the creation. A refrain of the services of the Church is heard in 11:26, "For God is a good God and He loves mankind." This is truly revelatory. The religions of the world were designed to placate angry, passionate, and irrational gods who might at any whim strike man down in fury. Sacrifices and religious actions were performed as a safety net against these gods and elemental forces. Yet the revealed God of Abraham is one who loves His creation, and as this passage finishes, corrects and warns man so that he may be freed from evil and united to his Creator. It is this contrast of the life-giving God of Wisdom against the death-dealing gods of paganism that the author will demonstrate.

From this point, the author continues his argument against idolatry. The futility and foolishness of idolatry is held up against the light of the revelation of the true God.

> But You, our God, are kind, true, patient,
> And govern all things in mercy.
> For even if we sin, we belong to You and know Your might;
> But we will not sin,
> Because we know that we are counted as belonging to You.
> For to know You is complete righteousness,
> And to know Your might is the root of immortality.

For neither have the evil practices of human art deceived us,
Nor a form stained with diverse colors,
The barren labor of painting,
Whose appearance creates a desire in fools
That longs for the lifeless form of a dead image. (15:1–5)

Once again in the midst of a discourse on idolatry, the revelation of the God of Abraham is held up against statues of wood, clay, and metal. God is life-giving and merciful in spite of sin. It is this very truth that drives man into the arms of God and toward righteousness. Idolatry desires to protect man from capricious deities that revel in death, but ironically it drives man further toward despair and destruction. It is a fool's errand. This passage again typifies the contrast the author uses in his argument against idolatry. Whereas in other wisdom literature, such as Proverbs, the opposite of wisdom is foolishness, in this book idolatry is the antithesis of wisdom. It may be that idolatry is the logical progression of foolishness. The book continues on this same path, and Egypt continues as the foil set in opposition to the life-giving God of Wisdom.

USE IN THE CHURCH

Because of the clear teaching concerning idolatry and wisdom, and the further revelation of Wisdom as Person, this book finds it way into the pages of the New Testament, the liturgy of the Church, and the writings of the Church Fathers.

Wisdom 2:12–20 is a clear prophecy of the Passion of Christ. This passage describes evil men plotting against the righteous man because of the guilt they feel. According to the evil men, the righteous man claims to have "knowledge of God," calls himself a "child of the Lord," and "pretends that God is his Father." The evil men attempt to test God by putting an end to the life of this righteous man, for "if the righteous man is a son of God, He will help him." But unfortunately for the wicked, they "did not know the mysteries of God."

Paul's discussion of idolatry and its results in Romans 1:19–32 shows a striking similarity to Wisdom 13:1–9 and 14:22–27.

Chapter 13 is part of the section on wisdom through history. The author moves from the specific example of the Egyptians at the time of Moses to the general example of all men: Man was unable to see beyond creation and come to the knowledge of God. Yet if they saw the beauty in creation, how much greater and more powerful is the Creator. The author concludes that man is without excuse, "For if they were able to know so much / With their ability to investigate the world, / How is it possible they did not quickly find / The Lord of all these things?" (13:9). Man's intelligence fails to move him beyond creation to the Creator, and he falls into worshipping himself or the creation around him.

Chapter 14 follows with the results of man's idolatry. Previously, man worshipped the creature rather than the Creator; now this idolatry leads to moral confusion. They hold "child-murdering rites . . . keep neither life nor marriages pure . . . and everything is mixed." Then a list of sinful actions is given, beginning with murder and ending in debauchery. But the central image in this list is most powerful—they are faulted with "confusion over what is good." This agrees with the author's conclusion about idolatry.

In Romans 1:19–32, according to Paul, God's invisible attributes are clearly seen, and thus man is without excuse. Yet they "changed the glory of the incorruptible God into an image made like corruptible man." As a result, God gave them up to uncleanness. Paul then lists a similar collection of vices that flow from the rejection of the life of God and the embrace of death-dealing idolatry.

Other passages in the New Testament that reflect verses in Wisdom are as follows:

1 Corinthians 2:7–12	Wisdom 9:13, 17
2 Corinthians 5:1–4	Wisdom 9:15
Ephesians 6:11–17	Wisdom 5:17–20
Hebrews 8:2–5	Wisdom 9:8

The Church uses Wisdom of Solomon passages as the Old Testament reading on several days throughout the liturgical year. The first one, from chapter 3, has already been discussed above; it is the reading for Vespers of the Sunday of All Saints.

The next reading is a collection of verses used on August 29 (Sept. 11 OS) for the Feast of the Beheading of St. John the Baptist. The reading is taken from 4:7, 16–17, 19—5:2. Found in the section on wisdom and eternal life, these verses examine the fate of the righteous and the wicked. Their destiny is often not discernible in this life, and in fact it may appear that the wicked has succeeded in his wickedness, while the righteous suffered unnecessarily because of his virtuous life.

The reading begins with a statement of faith: "But though a righteous man may die before his time, / He shall be at rest" (4:7). This becomes a guiding principle throughout, but is challenged by outward appearances, for the wicked may "see the end of the wise man, / But will not understand what the Lord purposed for him" (4:17). It is often not till the final judgment that the righteous will be vindicated, for here "the righteous man will stand with confidence . . . and [the wicked] shall be amazed at his unexpected salvation" (5:1, 2).

St. John the Baptist is a perfect image of these truths. He was imprisoned for speaking the truth to an apostate ruler, and later was beheaded as a result. Yet he is praised by Jesus as the greatest born among women. He is given a place of honor in Orthodoxy by being set directly left of Jesus on the iconostasis in Orthodox churches. Throughout history, St. John's relics have continued to perform miracles, up to this very day.

The final reading is also used on the Sunday of All Saints and is found in 5:15—6:3. Beginning with the declaration that the righteous live forever, the writer describes God's protection and care for the righteous man. God is portrayed as a warrior arming Himself for battle to defend the righteous. St. Paul's imagery of the Christian donning the armor of God hearkens back to this passage.

Then the rulers of the earth are warned to consider this picture of God. For those in power have greater opportunity to oppress the greatest number of people, and they must decide whether to follow the ephemeral hope of the wicked or the life-giving promises of the righteous. All men, regardless of position, should heed this call to righteousness.

The passage is read directly after 3:1–9 and supports the proposition that the righteous will live forever. In chapter 3, God upholds the righteous through struggles with evil, and in this passage God overwhelms evil with His might. The same truth is being told, but one passage is written from the earthly perspective of the righteous enduring the trials of life, and the other from the heavenly perspective of eternity guiding and holding the righteous in the care of God's right hand. This is the story of Pascha—one only arrives at the empty tomb through the cross and the grave. Read from the perspective of the Feast of All Saints, these passages provide a window into sainthood; it is a crucified life leading to resurrection.

Among the Fathers, the Christological and moral readings dominate their approach and commentary. The passage previously mentioned in chapter 2 regarding an image of the persecuted righteous man is fulfilled in the Person of Jesus Christ. This passage is referenced by Fathers of the Church such as Athanasius, Chrysostom, and Hippolytus in supporting the Old Testament witness for the Incarnation.

However, the last verse in this passage garners attention as well. Wisdom 2:24 states, "But death entered the world by the envy of the devil, / And those of his portion tempt it." Both John of Damascus[36] and Jerome[37] mention this, and it forms a large part of the Orthodox doctrine of salvation. Death is the enemy; Christ came to trample down death by death and bring life to mankind—and through man to all of creation. Likewise, a similar passage in 1:13 gives the positive expression of this understanding of death by proclaiming, "God did not make death, / Neither does He have pleasure over the destruction of the living." It was through the sin of man that death entered into the world, and continues to enter the world.

---

36 St. John of Damascus, An Exact Exposition of the Orthodox Faith: Book 3:1, Nicene and Post-Nicene Fathers Series 2, Volume 9, Philip Schaff (ed.), p. 45

37 St. Jerome, The Letters of St. Jerome: Letter 108, To Eustochium, Nicene and Post-Nicene Fathers Series 2, Volume 6, Philip Schaff (ed.), p. 204

The other major Christological passage in the book is 7:22–30. A description of wisdom is given in which it becomes apparent why the Fathers equated the Person of Christ with the Wisdom of God. The passage begins, "Wisdom is a spirit that is rational, / Holy, only-begotten." The phrase "only-begotten" is enough to tip off the reader to a foreshadowing of Christ. Later in the passage, we see that Wisdom is "the radiance of eternal light, / A spotless mirror of the operative power of God / And the image of His goodness" (7:26). Orthodox Christians hear in this echoes of the Nicene Creed, which proclaims Christ as "light of light, true God of true God." Gregory the Theologian, Ambrose, Basil the Great, Gregory of Nyssa, and Augustine are among the many Fathers who cite this passage as a reference to Christ. This passage is significant in the Orthodox defense of Christ as Eternal God as opposed to the Arian notion of Christ as creature.

The Wisdom of Solomon is tightly and artistically composed and is worthy of serious study and reflection. Christ is clearly encountered in this book through the Wisdom of God. The two paths of life and death appear as alternatives that each man must choose between, but the path of life can only be entered through the Wisdom of God.

 *The Wisdom of Sirach*

The Wisdom of Sirach is the longest book of wisdom literature in Scripture. Much like Proverbs, it is a collection of wise sayings and practical advice for applying the law of God or Torah to daily life. In Western Christianity, it is often referred to Ecclesiasticus, which means "the Church's book."

Like the other wisdom books, this book is difficult to outline or to fit within a firm structure. Many chapters seem unconnected with no transitions from one subject to another. At times it has the feeling of a jumbled collection of classroom lecture notes.

The most beneficial insights about the structure and purpose of the book are found in the Prologue. There we discover that this book is a compilation of the teachings of a famous Jewish scribe, Jesus ben Sirach. He was a teacher of the Law who wrote down many of his teachings, summaries, and applications of the Torah. Sirach's grandson gathered his grandfather's writings and translated them for Jews living outside their Hebrew-speaking homeland.

In the Prologue, the grandson informs the reader of the content of the book and his purpose behind its compilation. He states that these notes were originally written in Hebrew and he does his best to render them accurately in Greek. The translator was compiling this text for the Jews of the Greek-speaking world living in Egypt and around the Mediterranean. It appears the original notes were written around 180 BC but were not translated and published until 130 BC, making them very close to the time of Christ and the New Testamental period.

In spite of the difficulties involved in detecting a firm structure, I will attempt one that shows several of the major divisions in the book in order to help us gain a foothold of understanding that will allow us to apply Sirach's wisdom to our modern life.

Three major praises of wisdom are spaced through the book. The first is found in 1:1–18, the second in chapter 24, and the third in the last chapter. The praise of wisdom is a common feature in all the wisdom literature of Scripture, and because of the personification of wisdom, the identification with Christ becomes natural in the life of the Church. Another key division is in chapter 42, where Sirach saw creation as a vehicle for God's wisdom. Looking at the book along these seams shows a love for wisdom that praises the God of wisdom, leading men on a path to search for and embrace these truths in every facet of life. The lover of God unites himself with God by applying the mind of God to all aspects of life.

I. Prologue
II. First Praise of Wisdom with Warnings to the Wise and Instructions for Life (chs. 1–23)
III. Second Praise of Wisdom with Instructions for Life and Gratitude to God (24:1—42:14)
IV. Praise of God Working in Creation and Man (42:15—50:26)
V. Final Praise of Wisdom (ch. 51)

There are very few topics that Sirach does not cover. Friendship, leadership, the tongue, money, and marriage are mentioned repeatedly. Ultimately, all wisdom flows from God above through our union with Him, and Sirach intersperses this principle throughout his guidance.

The praises of wisdom provide a summary of all the varied material in the book. The first praise asserts that wisdom comes from God. God's Word is the fountain of wisdom, and only in Him is the fullness of wisdom found. Wisdom is poured forth into all creation from the throne of God, as a gift and expression of love to all mankind. Just as the Book of Proverbs connects the fear of the Lord with wisdom, so does Sirach. The fear of the Lord is the key that unlocks the door of wisdom for man. Yet this fear is not oppressive but leads to honor, glory, and rejoicing for man. Wisdom is foundational to the creation of man, and only the fear of the Lord brings the fullness of wisdom.

In the second praise section, wisdom is her own praise. She speaks in the presence of God and comes forth from the mouth of God. She is eternal, yet wanders throughout all creation looking for a place to rest. Rest is found through the people of Israel, as she is commanded by God to make her home among God's chosen people.

The author paints wisdom as a fruitful tree and vine that produces all good things. All men are invited to partake of the tree of wisdom. Those who hunger and thirst will be eternally satisfied by her. Those who obey will be protected from sin. Wisdom goes forth from her roots in Israel into all the earth for all mankind. On one hand, this is an Old Testament assertion of Israel's place among all nations as the one chosen to dispense wisdom and salvation to all mankind. On the other hand, this image is fulfilled through Christ, who comes forth bodily from the nation of Israel and is Wisdom Incarnate, saving all mankind through His life, death, and Resurrection.

The final praise of wisdom is a praise to God. Wisdom has delivered Sirach from death and destruction, and he praises God for it. Sirach sought wisdom from his youth and was supported by it throughout his life. Whether rich or poor, wisdom created an immeasurable value. In a verse that reminds the Christian reader of Jesus, the incarnation of Wisdom (Matt. 11:30), the author exhorts the reader to submit to the yoke of wisdom (51:26). For under this yoke the author has "found much rest for myself" (51:27).

Wisdom is shown as eternal, the Word of God, and essential to the creation of man. This leads the early Church to see wisdom and especially its personification as an expression of Jesus Christ, the Second Person of the Trinity. Wisdom saves and delivers from death. Wisdom follows man into the grave and raises him out of the clutches of Hades. Seen through the revelation of Jesus Christ, these passages are clearly images of man's salvation through Christ. Only by being united to Him can man have wisdom, because He is wisdom; He will protect us from sin and give us life.

SIRACH'S HALL OF FAME

Prior to Sirach's final praise of wisdom, he records a "Hall of Fame" of the godly in chapters 44–50. The New Testament Book of Hebrews contains a similar catalog of people of faith. The Wisdom of Solomon's Hall of Fame in chapter 10 teaches us to reject the foolishness of idolatry and embrace faith in the God of Israel. The list in Hebrews emphasizes the invisible nature of faith made manifest by the lives of men and women who believed in God, yet seemed foolish to the world around them. Ultimately, this was a faith that looked forward to a promise fulfilled in Christ.

Sirach begins his list of the faithful with Enoch, Noah, Abraham, Moses, and Aaron. He says of Abraham, "no one is found like him in glory. / He kept the law of the Most High" (44:19, 20). This is surprising because Abraham lived four hundred years prior to Moses' receipt of the written law of God. This stretch of time teaches the reader that the Torah is more than the written law; it encompasses faithfulness to God, which Abraham's life represents. Moses is honored as expected because he is faithful and gentle; and he delivered the law of life to Israel.

Sirach focuses more attention on Aaron. He praises Aaron not so much for his own achievements as for the blessings God bestowed on him. For to Aaron and his sons God entrusted the priesthood and the worship of God. Israel's worship was ordained by God and brought blessing to the people. Usurping the authority of the priesthood and the pattern of worship entrusted to Aaron is condemned. The story of the rebellious Dathan, Abiram, and Korah is referenced to further illustrate this point (Num. 16; 26).

Aaron's grandson, Phineas, is the next to be praised. He is a less well-known character in Scripture, but he showed zeal in the fear of the Lord. He stood fast when the people fell from God, and made atonement for Israel by re-establishing peace among the people.

During the wandering in the wilderness, Israel encountered the people of Moab and allowed themselves to be seduced by the women of that country. This seduction led them into idolatry, and they attached themselves to the false god Baal. Speaking through Moses, God commanded that all those consecrated to Baal be punished through death. Shockingly, an Israelite man and foreign woman brazenly came into the tabernacle, and although the text appears intentionally obscure, it appears they committed fornication in the presence of the full congregation. This behavior would have been a common worship practice among the pagan religions, but utterly abhorrent to the faith of Israel.

Phineas took a spear and threw it through the bodies of the man and woman. As a result of this spreading of pagan worship through-out the camp of Israel, a physical plague had infected the people. Phineas's defense of the worship of God stopped the plague. God honored Phineas and gave him an eternal priesthood because of the atonement he made for the people of Israel. His inclusion in this list stresses faithfulness to God in true worship, and that departure from true worship brings death.

Men such as Joshua and Caleb, the righteous judges, Samuel, the prophet Nathan, and King David are next to be praised because of their faithfulness to God and rejection of idolatry. King David defended the people in battle and honored the worship of Israel through the writing of the Psalms. His adulterous actions with Bath-sheba are referenced by mentioning the prophet Nathan, but David's repentance and acceptance of Nathan's chastisement atones for his sin.

Solomon is remembered for building the temple and showing great wisdom in his youth, yet he allowed his body to be enslaved by pagan women, which led him into idolatry. Sirach blames this behavior for the tragic division of the kingdom of Israel. The irony is that Sirach is following in the Solomonic wisdom tradition with this book; but even wise Solomon can be tarnished by departing from the faith of his fathers. This is a great warning to all who pick up Sirach's book.

The great prophets Elijah and Elisha of the rebellious Northern tribes come next in Sirach's survey of virtue. King Hezekiah and the prophet Isaiah are linked together, as are Josiah and Jeremiah. These men were faithful to God, and much of their lives was an exhortation to fellow Jews to return to the worship of the God of the covenant. After Josiah is recalled, Sirach restates the virtue of only three kings worthy of praise: David, Hezekiah, and Josiah. Again, Solomon is omitted in spite of the deposit of wisdom he left.

Sirach then refers to the prophets and men of the exile and return. Ezekiel prophesied along with the twelve minor prophets and brought hope to his people. Zerubbabel, Joshua, and Nehemiah all rebuilt and reestablished the temple and the city of Jerusalem. The deeds of other righteous men throughout history are also recounted once again—Enoch, Joseph, Shem, Seth, and Adam.

The final character, who receives most of the attention, is one unfamiliar to most modern readers of Scripture: Simon, the high priest. This Simon is known to history as Simon II or Simon the Just. His tenure as high priest lasted from 219–199 BC and would have been known to Sirach. Sirach would have seen Simon leading the people in worship. For his students, Simon is a recent example of the virtues Sirach is extolling and provides a model of godliness and faithfulness.

Simon repaired the temple and restored Jerusalem. He is upheld as the epitome and crown of the sons of Aaron, and in him we see an image of Christ as High Priest making the final offering before God whereby we continually partake. According to the Jewish Mishnah, his chief maxim was, "The world exists through three things: the Law, worship, and beneficence." It is those three virtues that summarize not only the life of Simon, but also the lives of all the men before him. In many ways, the wisdom in Sirach's teaching can be contained in those three virtues. Wisdom is found in behavior that flows from right teaching, correct worship, and love of fellow man.

Because of the space Sirach devotes to this praise of Jewish heroes, it warrants a discussion. The placement in the book suggests that the lives of these men embody the ideals and practices of wisdom found throughout the book. Faithfulness to God in worship, adherence to the Law in daily life, and charity to neighbor summarize the teaching of Sirach, and these men exemplify those qualities.

His encomium begins with a general word arguing that God established glory and majesty through these heroes. Through faithful men, God will be displayed and made known throughout the world. This concept sounds very Christian and evangelical because of the proclamation of the knowledge of God through humanity. Yet this is not foreign to the Old Testament. From the beginning, Scripture stresses more than once that man was made in God's image, and one of God's first commands was that man multiply and take this image throughout the world. This was the purpose for Israel's creation: to be a light to the world, so that the world might see its uniqueness and wisdom and flock to the worship of the one, true God.

Although this passage is a litany of renowned personalities, it is not just those who lived in public greatness who are praised, but also the anonymous whose bequest to mankind is the greatness they bestow through the lives of their children. These people may be forgotten by history, but they were determined to rear up a generation that would display God's glory and majesty throughout creation.

IN THE NEW TESTAMENT

The Wisdom of Sirach appears to have had a substantial influence on the New Testament. This should come as no surprise because of the nearness of this book's composition to the New Testamental period. Matthew and James seem to have relied heavily on the wording and thought of Sirach. These two books were written directly to Jewish audiences, and it would have been helpful to communicate the Gospel in familiar language and expressions. Matthew especially is writing to demonstrate that Jesus of Nazareth is the Messiah and therefore the fulfillment of the Law. The first-century Jewish interpretation of the Law would have been heavily influenced by Sirach's application of Torah.

The Sermon on the Mount in Matthew is full of similarities with Sirach. Jesus' Golden Rule can be found in Sirach 31:15: "Understand the things of your neighbor by your own, / And in every matter be considerate." In 7:8–10, the teacher counsels against presuming forgiveness. The teacher is instructing his students about the nature of sin and the danger of repeated sin. To sin repeatedly, expecting forgiveness, is detrimental to the soul, for a time will come when the act becomes bondage and the heart is hardened to the point that one will not seek forgiveness. The example given is the man who continues to sin but disregards the seriousness of his actions, because he says of God, "He will look upon the multitude of my gifts, / And when I bring an offering to God Most High, He will accept it" (7:9).

In a similar way, Jesus in His sermon teaches that before approaching God for forgiveness, we must reconcile with our neighbor (Matt 5:42–45). A heart unwilling to forgive is unable to receive forgiveness. A man who is not serious about turning from sin cannot receive release from the power of that sin. Sirach caps this teaching by reinforcing endurance in prayer and diligence in almsgiving, which are also contained in Jesus' teaching.

Sirach's influence is so pervasive that we cannot discuss every parallel passage. The following chart summarizes similarities between Sirach and the New Testament:

Sirach 1:10	1 Corinthians 2:9
Sirach 2:5	1 Peter 1:7
Sirach 5:11	James 1:19
Sirach 6:24–28	Matthew 6:7
Sirach 7:14	Matthew 11:28
Sirach 7:34	Romans 12:15
Sirach 10:14	Luke 1:52
Sirach 11:19	Luke 12:19
Sirach 15:11ff	James 1:13
Sirach 23:1, 4	Matthew 6:9; James 3:9
Sirach 24:19	Matthew 11:28–30
Sirach 28:1–7	Matthew 5:21–22; 18:23–25
Sirach 28:12	James 3:10
Sirach 33:12–13	Romans 9:20–21

Sirach 37:28   1 Corinthians 6:12
Sirach 51:23–27   Matthew 11:28

Sirach 23 contains a prayer for wisdom. Immediately upon reading it, the Orthodox Christian recalls the Lenten prayer of St. Ephrem: "O Lord and Master of my life, take from me the spirit of sloth, faintheartedness, lust of power, and idle talk; but give rather the spirit of chastity, humility, patience, and love to Thy servant. Yea, O Lord and King, grant me to see my own errors and not to judge my brothers. For blessed are You unto ages of ages. Amen."

The prayer of Sirach begins, "O Lord, Father and Master of my life" (23:1). He prays to be protected from his own words, and that his mind and heart would be disciplined to prevent him from falling into error. He asks to be turned from haughty eyes, which is a look of superiority on all he sees. His final request is deliverance from lust and gluttony. Both prayers describe the characteristics of the wise man. To pray with belief is to ask to be transformed into the image of Wisdom Himself.

For many Christians, the Book of Proverbs is part of a daily rule of spiritual reading due to its practical nature. Because of its simplicity and the ability to touch on every situation man encounters in a fallen world, Sirach should be considered and incorporated into regular reading as well. Very little in the book is obscure or confusing; it can be read by children and adults with great benefit. This book is so diverse that a simple introduction is difficult, and a longer commentary is truly needed to do the content justice.[38] Hopefully, this introduction whets an appetite for further study and reading, and the Wisdom of Sirach will become a part of your Christian walk.

---

38 For such a commentary, see *Wise Lives: Orthodox Christian Reflections on the Wisdom of Sirach,* by Patrick Henry Reardon (Conciliar Press, 2009).

 Baruch and the Epistle of Jeremiah

BACKGROUND & SUMMARY

We will discuss Baruch and the Epistle of Jeremiah together because of their close relationship. They both take place during the same time period, and in some versions of the Old Testament the Epistle of Jeremiah is included as chapter 6 of Baruch. In some listings of the books of the canon, these two books along with Lamentations are absorbed into the Book of Jeremiah.

Discovering the identity of Baruch is a good place to start a survey of these two books. Baruch was the scribe of the prophet Jeremiah and accompanied him throughout his ministry. It is impossible to understand the man Baruch without knowing about the prophet Jeremiah and his times.

Jeremiah's prophetic tenure lasted from 626 to 586 BC. The kings Josiah, Jehoahaz, Jehoiachim, Jehoiachin/Jeconiah, and the final king of Judah, Zedekiah, all reigned during his lifetime. Jeremiah lived and prophesied during the waning days of the Kingdom of Judah, and it was his task to warn the people of their impending destruction and the urgent need to repent. Jeremiah was unsuccessful in bringing the whole nation back to faith in the God of Abraham; however, there were those who listened, and Baruch was one of them.

Baruch is first mentioned as an assistant to Jeremiah during the reign of King Jehoiachin/Jeconiah. Throughout the remainder of Jeremiah's ministry, Baruch was his messenger and scribe, and often was the one to deliver Jeremiah's prophecies to the kings and nobles.

Prophet and scribe were eventually imprisoned together. During their imprisonment, Jerusalem was captured and destroyed by the Babylonian army. They watched as the nobility, the wealthy, and the educated were exiled into Babylon.

Jeremiah and Baruch were left among the remnant to minister during their time of grief. Many of the remnant forced Jeremiah and Baruch to go into Egypt from Judea, despite Jeremiah's warning against this action. This group may be the beginning of the Egyptian Jewish community that eventually produced the Septuagint. It is also the same group that we encountered in 3 Maccabees. Baruch eventually left Jeremiah and went to minister to the exiles in Babylon, carrying with him a letter from Jeremiah. That letter prompted the writing of this book.

The Book of Baruch is only five chapters. It takes place after the Book of Jeremiah is completed. From the beginning of Baruch, it is apparent that Jeremiah has composed another message to the exiles living in Babylon. Despite his people's continual rejection, Jeremiah will not forsake the responsibility and ministry given to him by God. He cares for the people even though they are in exile, and they still must be exhorted to hold fast to their covenant with their God.

Baruch is instructed to take this message to the exiles. The Book of Baruch is the record of the people's response to Jeremiah's message. The Epistle of Jeremiah most likely represents the prophecy of Jeremiah that Baruch delivered to the community of exiles.

Below is a basic outline and structure of the Book of Baruch:

I.   Introduction (1:1–4)
II.   People Respond in Prayer, Fasting, & Almsgiving (1:5–9)
III. Request for Prayer (1:10—2:10)
IV.   Confession in Prayer (2:11—3:8)
     1. Prayer for deliverance due to their sins (2:11–26)
     2. Remembrance of God's promises (2:27—3:8)
V.   Exhortation to Righteousness (3:9—5:9)
     1. Exhortation to the people in praise of wisdom
         (3:9—4:8)

Baruch begins with the Jewish exilic community in Babylon. The exiles and the former king Jeconiah (Jehoiachin) are present to hear the message that Baruch is to give. Baruch stands among the people to read a message "from the book." Remember that many of those to whom Baruch reads this prophecy would have knowledge of Jeremiah and Baruch. Many may have rejected the prophet's exhortations while in Jerusalem, but now, since many of the events he prophesied have come to pass, they are much more attentive to his words. This probably explains their immediate reaction to his message. Another thing to consider is that Daniel and his three friends Hananiah, Mishael, and Azariah (Shadrach, Meshach, and Abednego) were part of this exilic community and may have been among the audience that heard this message.

The content of Baruch does not consist of this "book" that Baruch reads to the people. Rather, it consists of the people's response to the message given. The identity of "the book" is a mystery. Several theories have been proposed.

One is that the book is the Torah, or at least a part of it, such as Deuteronomy. Within Holy Scripture there is a precedent for the reading of the Torah eliciting such a response. King Josiah found the Torah hidden in a wall during palace renovations. He was deeply moved by its word and had it read before the people, and the message caused them to return to their God. Later in history when the exiles returned, the priest Ezra read the Torah before the people and they responded in repentance.

Another possibility is the Book of Jeremiah. The people would have been familiar with the prophet, and Baruch would have been the scribe who wrote much of the book, so he would have had ready access to the prophecies of Jeremiah.

Finally, the message could be the writing known as the Epistle of Jeremiah. In the Septuagint, the Epistle comes after Baruch; and in many copies of the Old Testament, the Epistle is included as a sixth chapter of Baruch. We will eventually look at the contents of the Epistle, but because of the close connection between these two books, and the message of the Epistle compared with the response of the people, it seems that this is the best solution to the identity of the book Baruch reads. Baruch had been forced into Egypt along with Jeremiah, yet tradition does have Jeremiah sending Baruch to the exiles in Babylon. The beginning of the Epistle of Jeremiah makes clear that it was to be delivered to the Babylonian exiles, so the circumstances seem to lead to this last conclusion.

Upon hearing the word from Baruch, the people respond with weeping and the threefold pattern we have seen in other books among the Readables. Almsgiving, prayer, and fasting make up their response. They immediately pray and fast before the Lord and collect money to send back to the remnant in Jerusalem. The money is to be used for sin offerings and prayers for themselves and for King Nebuchadnezzar, their oppressor. The prayer requested along with alms is recorded: it is a confession of the sins of the exiles, a prayer for deliverance, and a remembrance of the promises of God.

Then, in 3:9, the tone shifts from prayer to a message of exhortation, apparently from Baruch, to know and embrace wisdom. In this we see in summary themes similar to those the Wisdom of Solomon and Sirach explored. Wisdom is to be sought and embraced. In wisdom light and life are found.

Baruch then concludes this book with a word of prophecy through the voice of Jerusalem. Jerusalem is personified and cries out to her children in exile. Her exhortation is one of courage. Even though the exile is a result of the sin of Israel, she still pleads with her children to be of good courage and remember that the Lord will ultimately deliver them. For the people can trust that "the One who brought these calamities upon you will bring you everlasting joy with your salvation" (4:29).

The remainder of the book is a response to Jerusalem's cry to her children. A message of hope and comfort is offered to Jerusalem. Just as she asked her children to be courageous, she is now asked to "take courage." The Eternal One of Israel will restore her children. Historically, this was fulfilled. The exiles remained in Babylon for seventy years, but returned, as we have read in Ezra. Jerusalem is to look eastward for her children and the joy that is coming. The message is true for us as Christians. For we worship toward the east, looking for the joy of Christ, who promised to return in the east and end the exile of this world.

USE IN THE CHURCH
Even though a small book, Baruch has liturgical uses in the Church. The man Baruch is also commemorated by the Church on September 28 (October 11 OS). Here is a selection of hymns for his feast day.

> *Apolytikion in the Fourth Tone*
> Thou didst foretell the Lord's divine Incarnation when thou didst cry out to the whole world, O Prophet: This is our God, there shall be none compared to Him; He was seen upon the earth, being born of a Virgin: He hath shone upon our souls the divine light of knowledge. And He doth grant salvation unto all who sing thy praise, O divinely inspired Baruch.

> *Kontakion in the Second Tone*
> As thou wast vouchsafed the shining rays of prophecy, thou also wast bound to Jeremias as his friend, and foretoldest of the Word's self-abasement for our refashioning, O all-lauded Prophet Baruch. Entreat Him to save us all, who honor thee.

The hymnology points us to the readings the Church uses from Baruch, and gives a hint as to the way the Church reads and understands these Scriptures through the light of Christ.

Baruch 3:36—4:4 is read on Nativity Eve. Before we hear the passage, the context in which it is read should tell us that within the pages of Baruch is a prophecy or foreshadowing of the Incarnation and the coming of Christ to the world. This passage comes at the end of Baruch's exhortation to the people and immediately before mother Jerusalem cries out for her exiled children.

This is our God; no other shall be compared to Him. He found the whole way of knowledge and gave it to Jacob His servant and to Israel His beloved. Afterwards, He was seen upon the earth and lived among men. She [wisdom] is the book of the commandments of God and the law that endures forever. All those who keep her will live, but those forsaking her will die. Return, O Jacob, and take hold of her. Walk toward the radiance of the presence of her light. Do not give your glory to another or the things that are of advantage to you to a foreign nation. O Israel, we are blessed, for what is pleasing to our God is known to us. (3:36—4:4)

God has given His law, covenant, and promises to Israel and then demonstrates the law to His people by becoming one of them. The Church seized upon the phrase, "He was seen upon the earth and lived among men." For it seems obvious in the light of Christ that the Incarnation is being prophesied. Christ is the Book and the Law incarnate, and in Him there is life. The last line is significant in light of the birth of Christ. The Church has come to celebrate God becoming man and revealing Himself to us in the manger at Bethlehem. The Church, the New Israel, is blessed, for the Incarnation, which "is pleasing to our God," is known to us; and this is cause for rejoicing.

Church Fathers such as Ambrose, Cyprian, Chrysostom, Gregory the Theologian, Cyril, Basil, and Hilary all commented in this way on this passage, but two particular comments stand out. St. John Cassian, in his work against the heretic Nestorius, quotes Baruch 3:37–38 and comments:

"This is," then, he says, "our God." You see how the prophet points to God as it were with his hand, and indicates Him as it were with his finger. "This is," he says, "our God." Tell me then, who was it that the prophet showed by these signs and tokens to be God? Surely it was not the Father? For what need was there that He should be pointed out, whom all believed that they knew? For even then the Jews were not ignorant of God, for they were living under God's law. But he was clearly aiming at this, that they might come to know the Son of God as God. And so excellently did the Prophet say that He who had found out all knowledge, i.e., had given the law, was to be seen upon earth, i.e., was to come in the flesh, in order that, as the Jews did not doubt that He who had given the law was God, they might recognize that He who was to come in the flesh was God, especially since they heard that He, in whom they believed as God the giver of the law, was to be seen among men by taking upon Him manhood, as He Himself promises His own advent by the prophet: "For I myself that spoke, behold I am here."[39]

So the one who gave the Law is Christ, and it was He who came and lived among men. St. Gregory of Nyssa quotes this passage to affirm that Christ came so that man may clearly know God. By becoming man, man could see God in a way that he was only able to conjecture previously. St. Gregory writes:

He, I say, appeared on earth and "conversed with men" that men might no longer have opinions according to their own notions about the Self-existent, formulating into a doctrine the hints that come to them from vague conjectures, but that we might be convinced that God has truly been manifested in the flesh, and believe that to be the only true "mystery of godliness."[40]

IN THE NEW TESTAMENT

Baruch is not quoted directly by the New Testament, yet there are a couple of passages that may be influenced by it. In Baruch 4:7, when

---

39 St. John Cassian, The Seven Books of John Cassian on the Incarnation of the Lord, Book 4, Chapter 9, Nicene and Post-Nicene Fathers Series 2, Volume 11, Philip Schaff (ed.), p. 578

40 St. Gregory of Nyssa, Against Eunomius, Book 2, Chapter 1, Nicene and Post-Nicene Fathers Series 2, Volume 5, Philip Schaff (ed.), p. 101

Jerusalem speaks of the sins of Israel, she equates the false idols of pagans with demons or devils. This idea was not new to Israel, but is found in the Torah. Deuteronomy 32:17, speaking of Israel's periodic apostasy, says, "They sacrificed to demons, not to God." Baruch is surely drawing from this passage.

St. Paul, in his discussion of the Eucharist in 1 Corinthians 10:14–21, speaks also of pagan idolatry. He likewise does not dismiss the idols as harmless and nothing, but says, "they sacrifice to demons and not to God."

Matthew 8:11 also bears relation to Baruch 4:37: "Behold, your sons whom you sent away are coming, gathered together from the east to the west by the word of the Holy One, rejoicing in the glory of God." Baruch is comforting the earthly Jerusalem with the return of her scattered children from both the east and the west. Matthew uses this idea of God gathering His children from the east and the west together at the end of time in the heavenly Jerusalem.

A final example is from the Gospel of John. In John 3:13, Jesus is speaking to Nicodemus about the Kingdom of God. Jesus tells him that no man has ascended into heaven to grasp the mysteries present there, and only He has authority to speak of these things because He has descended from the place of heavenly mysteries. Baruch 3:29 says, "Who has gone up into heaven and taken hold of her, and brought her down from the clouds." Baruch is speaking of the wisdom of God, who we know is the Person of Jesus Christ. And even in a veiled understanding, Baruch knows that no man has approached the wisdom of God, for this is only possible through the revelation of God. Jesus Christ is the perfect revelation of the wisdom of God to man, for He is the Wisdom of God made flesh.

Baruch is a small book, yet one the Church has chosen to use in her liturgy to proclaim the Incarnation of Christ. Like many of the other books we have studied, Baruch upholds the wisdom of God as the path of life. Israel's exile from Jerusalem can become an object lesson of this truth. To reject the worship and wisdom of God for the ways of the world and the idolatry of the nations is to embrace the way of death.

THE EPISTLE OF JEREMIAH

This short work keeps company with Obadiah, Jude, and Philemon as a one-chapter book of the Bible. Because of its brevity and connection with Baruch, many OT copies include it as the sixth chapter of Baruch. However, as with much of Scripture, brevity does not necessarily translate into lack of content.

The first few verses explain the purpose and direction of the letter. Jeremiah wrote to the exiles who had recently been taken to Babylon. As explained previously, these circumstances make the Epistle the perfect candidate for "the book" Baruch read to the exiles. Upon hearing the words, the people repented of their sins and sought the face of God for atonement.

As we will see, this letter is designed to elicit repentance, because Jeremiah is explaining to the people the reason for their exile and ultimately the way out of exile. The reason was the rejection of their covenant relationship with God and their continual wandering after pagan gods. This neglect of the Torah leads to the natural deathlike consequences of the Exile.

Idolatry is the cause of their exile, yet physical exile is but a manifestation of the condition of their heart. The hearts of the people had been separated from their God long before they were physically removed from His city. Jeremiah creates an argument that explains the death-inducing nature of idolatry, its corruption and destruction of men who allow themselves to be shaped in the idol's likeness rather than the likeness of their God. Below is a simplified outline of the book (the reader will find overlap and integration throughout):

I.   Introduction and Explanation of the Reasons for Exile (1–7)
II. Warning Against Idolatry (8–72)
     1. Idols are a disgrace (8–38)
     2. Idols make man a disgrace (39–72)
III. Freedom from Idolatry Protects from Disgrace (73)

Idolatry and rejection of the God of Israel was the major reason the Israelites ended up in exile, and idolatry will be the major temptation during exile. The Babylonians will carry their gods in procession and the people will display fear, but fear must not seize the hearts of the exiles. In their hearts, they must cry out, "'One must worship You, O Lord.' For [God's] angel is with all of you, and he is searching your souls" (5, 6).

Hippolytus quotes this passage in his treatise on the Lord's Prayer, insisting that prayer should not be mere words, but must penetrate the entire inner man and flow from within. Such is Jeremiah's command; the worship of the One God must be ingrained within their hearts if they are to stand against the idolatry of Babylon. One can imagine Daniel and his companions hearing these words with open hearts, so that this phrase becomes a standard of faith during their exile. In later years, gods were displayed and the people bowed. Yet the three holy youths refused and were cast into the fiery furnace. As promised by Jeremiah, God's Angel was present and delivered them.

The recurring phrase in the remainder of the book is, "Do not fear them." Jeremiah gives multiple reasons and repeats this command five times. Idols are seen as dumb and deaf, needing man for their protection and caretaking. They cannot protect or rule, even though they may hold scepters or weapons. During times of war, the hypocrisy of the pagan priest is on display when he slinks away to protect the idols from destruction, yet is really securing his own life in a hidden place of safety. The connection between prostitution and idolatry demonstrates the lack of righteousness of the idol-worshipping man. Rather than righteousness, he inherits corruption.

Jeremiah's final word is intended to bolster the faith of the exiles: "Better therefore is a man who is righteous and has no idols, for he shall be far from disgrace." In a land where the faith of Abraham is held by a minority, the pressure to conform to local idolatry could be overwhelming. Judging from the story of the three youths in the furnace, many did follow the easy path of idolatry. The young men were obviously in the minority. To disregard the customs of the Babylonians could bring reproach, shame, and disgrace on one's family and tribe among the Gentiles. Yet Jeremiah reminds his people that they will be free from disgrace if they cleave to God. To be righteous may bring reproach from the world, but man's eternal soul stays free from disgrace, for rather than being shaped in the likeness of idols, he is conformed to the image and likeness of God.

The words of Elder Paisios summarize the heart of this book:

> Some people give their whole self to material things. They spend the entire day trying to do a job well, and do not think of God at all. We should not end up there. . . . You should not give all of your being—all of your energy and heart—to material things. This way, one becomes a pagan—an idol worshipper. Do your best at work, but do not give your heart to the work you do; give only your hands, your mind. Do not give your heart to hopeless, useless things. If you do, then how will your heart leap for Christ? When the heart is with Christ, then even the work we do is sanctified, our soul is at rest and there is real joy in our heart. Make the most of your heart, do not waste it. (Elder Paisios the Athonite)

 *Additions to Daniel: Susanna, Songs of the Three Holy Children, Bel & the Dragon*

The Book of the Prophet Daniel is found in all Old Testament canons, but much like the Book of Esther, the Greek version of Daniel includes prayers and stories that are not found in the modern Hebrew versions. Often, when these sections are included in an English Bible, they will be treated as separate and placed in an appendix or between the testaments. Yet in the Septuagint, they are an integral part of the Book of Daniel, and should be read as such.

The additions include two historical narratives referred to as "Susanna" and "Bel and the Serpent (Dragon)," which cap the beginning and end of the book respectively. The third addition is referred to as the "Songs of the Three Holy Children." These are hymns sung by the three young friends of Daniel who were thrown into the fiery furnace. In reality, these songs are comprised of two different hymns, one of which is sung by the Three Youths in unison and the second by the youth Azariah. These songs are an important part of the Orthodox liturgical tradition.

Rather than looking at these additions sequentially, we will consider them according to genre—the historical accounts first and then the hymns.

SUSANNA

The portions known as "Susanna" and "Bel and the Serpent" constitute a wonderful prologue and epilogue to the Book of Daniel. As a prologue, Susanna introduces the person of Daniel to the reader. Daniel in this account is a young boy. It is through Susanna's story that we encounter him and begin to sense his nature and importance as a prophet of God. Even though Daniel appears and is critical to the resolution, the focus is on Susanna and her virtue.

The story takes place among the exiled community of the Jews in Babylon. Susanna is the wife of a wealthy Jew named Jehoiakim. One has to wonder whether Jehoiakim was part of the Davidic nobility that had been carried off into Babylon and allowed to retain some of their wealth. Susanna herself was from righteous parents who had instilled the Law of Moses into her heart. She was known for her beauty and fear of the Lord.

Susanna's house was adjoined by a spacious garden that contained relaxing baths. Two elders had been appointed by the Jews to help govern their community; we learn early on that these men are viewed as unrighteous by the Lord. The elders watched Susanna go into her garden daily and began to desire her (8, 9). They strategized how they could get her alone and take advantage of her. One day they hid in the garden before she came out to bathe. When her maids left, they appeared and tried to force her to lie with them (20–23). Susanna cried out and the servants came, but the elders fabricated a tale that made Susanna look like a guilty adulteress.

The next day, the people assembled to judge the case and condemn her to death. She cried out to God (42ff), and God heard her prayer. Daniel, a young boy (twelve years old, according to St. Ignatius), appeared and spoke, clearly proclaiming God's voice (46ff). Daniel judged the case by questioning the elders separately and catching them in their lies. The whole assembly rejoiced and blessed God. The elders were then put to death. Susanna was vindicated because "nothing shameful was found in her." Daniel as well gained a "great reputation" among his people.

From this prologue, we learn that this man Daniel is a man of wisdom. The childlike purity of his heart is able to see God; and we can expect that he will hear and report the voice of God through the remainder of the book. Also, Daniel is a deliverer. Just as Susanna was rescued from certain shame and death, others will be saved through the influence and person of Daniel. Reading through New Testament eyes, Daniel becomes a type of Christ, whose purity of heart and willingness to suffer delivers those around him. Not only is the man Daniel introduced, but these themes of prophecy, discernment, wisdom, and deliverance can be found throughout the book.

On the surface, this is a wonderful story that mirrors many accounts in Scripture. A virtuous person is placed in a situation of peril from which there is no escape without comprising his or her faith in God. St. Ambrose acknowledges this with Susanna: "[for] when threatened with the fear of false witness, seeing herself hard pressed on one side by danger, on the other by disgrace, preferred to avoid disgrace by a virtuous death rather than to endure and live a shameful life in the desire to save herself."[41] The virtuous person chooses to face harm and destruction rather than succumbing to darkness. Then, at the point of deepest despair, he or she is rescued and vindicated before all. The story of Joseph in Genesis provides several examples of this.

The moral application is clear: Faithfulness is worth facing death, and a faithful death always ends in resurrection. This may not always be apparent in the short term, as in Susanna's case, yet these stories point to a future vindication that may be beyond this earthly existence. How many times do we encounter sin leading to our death, yet we succumb so that our position, reputation, wealth, and comfort may remain intact?

USE IN THE CHURCH

From early times in Christian history, Susanna was celebrated as a figure to be emulated. Susanna is depicted in early Church iconography in murals gracing the walls of places of worship. She is celebrated in the Church on December 19 (January 2). A wide variety of Church Fathers use her as an example of chastity, perseverance, and virtue.

St. Hippolytus taps into something deeper than the surface or

---

41   St. Ambrose, On the Duties of Clergy, Book 3, Chapter 14:90, Nicene and Post-Nicene Fathers Series 2, Volume 10, Philip Schaff (ed.), p. 82

moral understandings in his reading of the text.[42] Susanna, like so many virtuous women of the Old Testament, typifies the Church, and her husband then is a type of Christ. The garden where they dwell is "the calling of the saints, who are planted like fruitful trees in the Church." The garden is located in Babylon, which is usually a type of the world, for their garden was in the world but not of it. The two elders who falsely accuse Susanna are types of the two peoples that persecute the Church. For Hippolytus, these would have been the pagan Romans and the Jewish community.

In addition to such typological significance, Susanna's story points to the journey man must make in union with God. The bath in the garden and the anointing with oil are images of the two mysteries that usher one into the Kingdom of God. Shortly after her initiation, Susanna experiences temptation in the garden like her foremother Eve. This follows also the pattern and way that Christ laid down for the faithful. Immediately after His baptism, he was assaulted by temptation. Susanna refuses the temptation and stands firm in her faith, is saved from certain death, and experiences resurrection through Daniel, who is a type of Christ for her. This pattern of death, resurrection, and union with God not only occurs in the initial steps of baptism, chrismation, and the Eucharist, but is a pattern whereby the Christian lives. Each day should be an experience of little deaths and resurrections that conform us more and more into the likeness of God.

BEL AND THE DRAGON

As Susanna provided the prologue to Daniel, Bel and the Dragon could be considered the epilogue to the book. Susanna introduced the reader to the person of Daniel and set the stage for his prophetic mission. Bel summarizes many of the themes that are found within the book. In this account, Daniel is an old man at the end of his prophetic life, but God is still using him as a deliverer and defender of

---

42 St. Hippolytus, On Daniel, Chapter 6:10, Ante-Nicene Fathers, Volume 5, Philip Schaff (ed.), pp. 191, 192

the truth. Daniel has experienced much in life, from exile to government prominence. Kingdoms have risen and fallen around him, and in each one he was persecuted and revered, but he continued to be faithful to his God.

At this point in the book, Daniel is once again the confidant of a king, the Persian king Cyrus. The Babylonians had an idol named Bel. Every day large amounts of food and wine were offered to the idol, and then it would be gone the next day. As a result, the king worshiped Bel and questioned Daniel about his own religious beliefs.

Daniel approached the king and told him he was being deceived. He devised a test to prove the deception. That evening, the house of Bel was sealed shut after the food and wine were offered, so no one could enter and steal the food during the night. If the food was gone the next morning, then Bel would be seen as a god.

We are told there was a secret passage under the statue through which the priests and their families would sneak into the temple and feast each night. Daniel must have suspected this, because he had servants sprinkle ashes on the floor of the temple before it was closed for the night. Upon rising the next morning, the king discovered the footprints, seized the priests and their families, and had them executed.

In the pagan temple was also a large serpent that the people worshipped. The king questioned Daniel about the truth of this idol. Daniel asked the king for permission to slay the serpent without using his sword or staff. The king granted permission. Daniel made cakes of pitch, tar, and hair and put them in the mouth of the serpent. The serpent ate the food, burst open, and died, angering the people who worshipped it. The king was forced to give Daniel over to the mob, and he was thrown once more into the lion's den. These lions were left unfed for the six days Daniel was with them.

The story shifts from Daniel's plight, and we are taken to Judea, where the prophet Habakkuk is cooking stew. The angel of the Lord speaks to Habakkuk and commands him to take the stew to Daniel in the lions' den in Babylon. The angel then carries Habakkuk by the hair of his head to the den, where he delivers the meal to Daniel.

On the seventh day, the king opens the den, finds Daniel alive, and praises the God of Daniel.

The follies of idolatry are exposed once more in this story. If there is one theme that comes from the time of Exile, it is the rejection of idolatry. It was a reason for the Exile, and the time in Babylon provided a constant reminder of this folly.

This story also summarizes much of the life of Daniel. On one hand, due to his wisdom and virtue, he always grew into an advisory role to every king, regardless of the kingdom or administration. However, in this capacity his faith was always tested, and Daniel was forced to choose death over faithlessness. In each case he becomes an image of the resurrection. He is condemned to die, but through the power of God he is brought back to the land of the living. Even the prophecies of his book speak to this theme. Regardless of the plight of mankind and its kingdoms, God is victorious and ultimately proves to be sovereign over all His creation.

Very little is said among the Fathers regarding this story. Cyril of Jerusalem and Athanasius mention the book in passing in discussing various subjects. St. Cyril refers to Habbakuk's transportation to the lion's den in discussing the rationality of the ascension of Christ. St. Irenaeus speaks of it at greater length. St. Irenaeus's unique ministry in the early Church was to defend Orthodox Christianity from heresy, and often this heresy took the form of some gnostic sect. It is not surprising that he would draw from anti-idolatrous texts to witness to the living God rather than the false images created by heretics.[43]

PRAYER OF AZARIAH /
SONG OF THE THREE HOLY YOUTHS
SUMMARY

In the middle of chapter 3 of Daniel we find hymns and prayers that have been prayed and sung by the Church since early times. These

---

43 St. Irenaeus, Against Heresies, Book 4:5, Ante-Nicene Fathers, Volume 1, Philip Schaff (ed.), pp. 466-67

expressions of deep felt prayer pour forth from the hearts of the Three Holy Youths. This is the name given in the Church to the young men known as Shadrach, Meschach, and Abednego. This is a familiar story to most Christians, but their prayers are unknown to many.

King Nebuchadnezzar erected a golden idol and commanded all his people to bow down and publicly worship this false god. In spite of the mass obedience and intense pressure to conform, these youths refused to bow before anything but the God of Abraham. This refusal angered the king, and the three were thrown into a superheated furnace. It was stoked to such a temperature that the workers died from the heat. Yet the three youths were untouched by the flames, and a mysterious fourth man appeared in the furnace with them. This figure is believed by the Church to be a preincarnate appearance of the Son of God. His appearance saved the three young men.

In the midst of the fire, they compose and sing two hymns in praise and repentance to the God of Heaven. One is by Azariah (Meschach) alone, and the second hymn is from the mouths of all three. The first hymn is sung as they enter the fire and face certain death; the second is sung within the fire after they have been delivered by the Son of God. Let us look at each hymn individually and then see how they have been used by the Church.

SONG OF AZARIAH

As the young men are thrown into the furnace, their minds must be overwhelmed with the prospect of pain, fear, and certain death. But one of them, Azariah, raises his voice in prayer to God. They could easily have directed blame and anger toward their God, for it was through obedience to Him they found themselves in the flames of death. But Azariah's immediate response displays the attitude of his heart. Below is a simple outline of his prayer:

I.   The Lord God Is Righteous in Everything He Has Done (26–33)

      1.   God is righteous in all things (26–27)

     2.   Righteous in His judgment of Jerusalem (28–31)
- a.   Because of their sin
- b.   Because of disobedience

     3.   Righteous in His deliverance of the Jews to pagans (32–33)

II.   Don't Deliver Us Completely to the Enemy (34–42)

     1.   Because of Your promises

     2.   We will be a sacrifice

     3.   We will completely follow You

III.   Deliver Us (43–45)

Azariah begins by praising God and proclaiming His righteous judgment on all things. The circumstance of their impending martyrdom is part of his praise of God's sovereignty. Also, Azariah mentions the destruction of Jerusalem and their capture by pagans as righteous judgments of God. In doing so, he offers up a confession of sin and enumerates all the failings and wanderings Israel perpetrated against their God.

In no way would today's reader ascribe blame for Israel's plight to Azariah and his friends, but Azariah sees himself in the sins of Israel. It is because of this he can make this confession on behalf of the people. Chrysostom sees in his confession, "we sinned and acted lawlessly . . . we sinned in every way," a display of his virtues in knowing his distance from God. This is similar to the confession of the publican in his cry, "God have mercy on me a sinner"; or even Paul's assertion that he was the chief of sinners. Jerome also sees a moral understanding of this confession. In each human life, turmoil, restlessness, and passion blaze and suffocate the spirit of man; yet when a person cries out to the Lord, God will descend and extinguish the flame before it can penetrate the innermost part of the soul.

Yet in spite of all these happenings, Azariah implores God that the circumstances be merely for chastening and not total annihilation. He remembers the covenant promises God made to his forefathers as assurances of God's faithfulness to maintain the people of Israel. Azariah offers himself and his companions up to God as sacrifices on behalf of the people. The worship of Israel had become corrupted, and exile from the temple made it incomplete. Yet Azariah offers himself totally to God as an act of pure worship.

Sacrifice is merely a physical expression of worship. It is an expression of a person giving his whole being to God in the form of the alms or animal being offered. Here, Azariah is becoming the sacrifice on behalf of those whose sin and situation prevented pure worship. The completeness of this sacrifice is evident in the expression of total commitment to God. In this sacrifice, Azariah and his friends become images of the true sacrifice of pure worship Christ will offer on the Cross on behalf of all mankind. Perhaps it is this total unity with God in worship and sacrifice that prompts the Son of God to manifest Himself in the midst of the young men. Azariah concludes his song of prayer with a request for deliverance. God delivers them, but through the furnace. God still delivers man, but through the Cross.

This prayer should become every Christian's prayer, for all men face fire and turmoil in their lives. St. Jerome sees this as a necessary prayer for spiritual growth: "Whenever we are oppressed by various difficulties, let us repeat this same prayer with our whole heart. And whatever may happen to us, let us confess that it is only right that we endure it."[44]

NARRATIVE

Between the two hymns, a short narrative is inserted, lest we forget the severity of the young men's plight. The king's servants stoke the fire hotter, killing those surrounding the furnace. The presence of the Angel of the Lord is announced as He descends into the furnace to shake off "the fiery flame of the furnace." The Lord made the fire to be as a "dew-laden breeze" upon the bodies of the young men. The deliverance Azariah cried for in his song is fulfilled in these short verses. The hymn of the three together is a response to their salvation by the Angel of the Lord as they sing with one voice.

---

44 St. Jerome, *Jerome's Commentary on Daniel* 3:26-28a, translated by G.L. Archer Jr., Grand Rapids: Baker, 1977

SONG OF THE THREE YOUTHS

This hymn is a praise to God for all things. In reading this passage, one would be hard pressed to find some aspect of creation not listed. The structure follows a hierarchy that seems loosely based on the order of creation in Genesis.

The hymn begins with praise of God, the Creator and Lord of all. God is sitting upon His throne in His heavenly temple, and from there He is praised by all creation. The young men function as priests of creation, offering all that God made back to Him in praise. This is an essential aspect of man's nature and is evident in Genesis, when God commands Adam to name the animals and to be a steward of all creation. This priestly function is fulfilled perfectly in the celebration of the Eucharist, when the sacramental priest calls out, "Thine Own of Thine Own, we offer unto Thee, on behalf of all and for all." The royal priesthood (the laity) then responds, "We hymn Thee, we bless Thee, we give thanks to Thee, O Lord, and we pray to Thee, O our God."

Offering creation back to God in thanksgiving and praise is the heart of this hymn. For after praising God, these men call all creation to offer up praise to God. They begin with the heavenly hosts, then proceed to the sun and moon, all things in the heaven including the weather, then the various parts of the earth, the sea creatures, the birds of the air, and the earthbound animals—just as the days of creation move from the heavens to the earth, the animals, and then man.

The three youths call upon all men to praise God. From there they become more specific, finally coming back to themselves, whom they command to offer praise. They begin with all men, then move to God's people Israel, the priests, servants of God, the righteous departed, all holy and humble hearts, and finally themselves. Ending the hymn by exhorting their own hearts to praise and thank God demonstrates their own humility and desire to be faithful to their God forever. After they are removed from the furnace by an astonished Nebuchadnezzar, the pagan king follows their lead and offers thanks by saying, "Blessed is the God of Shadrach, Meshach, and Abednego" (3:95).

This hymn is no novel creation of three young men who

spontaneously rejoice in their deliverance, but an indication that Scripture had penetrated their hearts and naturally poured forth from them in praise. The phrase, "Give thanks to Him; for His mercy endures forever," which is the central theme of this song, is found throughout the OT, especially in the Psalms. King David first uses this phrase in praise to God for bringing the ark into Jerusalem in 1 Chronicles 16:34. King Solomon responds in kind when the ark is brought into the temple and God's presence is manifest (2 Chronicles 5:13). Psalms 105, 106, 117, and 135 use this refrain again and again. Jeremiah 40:11 prophesies that after the desolation of Jerusalem, one day God's people will return and cry out this refrain once more. It was not long after Jeremiah's time that the young men voiced this praise in the furnace. A generation later, when Ezra led the remnant to rebuild the temple among the ruins of Jerusalem, they cried out "to the Lord that He is good, that His mercy is upon Israel forever" (2 Ezra 3:11).

USE IN THE CHURCH

Christ is present in these hymns and this story of the three in the furnace. The obvious image of Christ is the fourth man in the furnace. This is the Angel of the Lord, and the Church has always seen these appearances of the Angel within the OT as a preincarnate appearance of the Son of God. He is the Deliverer and the One who saves His people from death. He does not save from afar but enters into their story and lives in order to save. The ultimate expression of this is the Incarnation and events of the Passion.

The deliverance of the three youths foreshadows the crucial events of our salvation—the Cross, the grave, and the third-day Resurrection. The innocent men were united with the Cross through their own martyrdom, and the furnace imaged the grave and Hades. For in their song, they cried out, "He delivered us from Hades / and saved us from the hand of death" (3:88). Christ pulls them from Hades once more into life as they are saved out of the furnace. This is one of the hymns the Church reads on Holy Saturday when Christ's descent into Hades is remembered.

Azariah functions as a type of Christ as well. He is an innocent man being martyred for his faithfulness to God, and he cries out in his prayer that he be accepted as a sacrifice to God for the people of Israel (3:38–40). Christ is the ultimate offering to God in pure worship, which no man could accomplish; but we are able to enter into that sacrifice at each Liturgy as we receive the Body and Blood of Christ.

Other images are present here as well. The Church points these out throughout her hymnography. The fiery furnace, just like the burning bush of Moses, becomes a repeated image of the Theotokos. She receives the fire of the Divinity into her womb but is not consumed. The Church sings, "We the faithful recognize in you, O Theotokos, the spiritual furnace, and just as He saved the three youths, the Most High has renewed the entire world in your womb" (Hymn of Matins). An image of the Trinity is manifest, as the Church sings in Matins: "Let us praise the divinity of three flames, one light shining from a single nature in three persons. The Father without beginning, the Word who is of the same nature as the Father, and the consubstantial Spirit who reigns with Him. O youths, bless your Creator and Redeemer, praise Him, you priests, and all you people, exalt Him forever!"

The Eucharist can also be seen here, for whenever we receive the Body and Blood, we are receiving the fire of the Godhead into our own person. This fire can be to condemnation if we partake unworthily; but when our hearts are prepared, the fire becomes like dew in our hearts, cleansing and restoring us.

These two hymns have become an integral part of Orthodox worship. Nine scriptural hymns form the basis for the Matins Canon, eight of which are found in the Old Testament. These two hymns from the Book of Daniel are the foundation for the seventh and eighth odes. As a result, every feast and matins service contains references to this account in Daniel, showing how the events in the furnace relate to the glory of God and the salvation of mankind.

Daniel and the Three Holy Youths are commemorated in the Church on December 17, shortly before the celebration of the

Incarnation on December 25. The hymns for these young men reference these events:

> *Troparion of the Holy Prophet Daniel and the*
> *Three Children (Tone 4)*
> Great are the achievements of faith! In the fountain of flame, as in refreshing water, the Three Holy Children rejoiced. And the Prophet Daniel proved a shepherd of lions as of sheep. By their prayers, O Christ our God, save our souls.

> *Kontakion of the Three Children in Babylon (Tone 2)*
> An image made with hands you would not worship, O thrice-blessed three; but protected by the ineffable Essence you were glorified in your ordeal by fire. From the midst of the devouring flames you called upon God, crying: Hasten, O compassionate One, in Thy mercy come to our aid, for if Thou willest Thou canst.

These stories and hymns we have discussed deepen the Christian's experience of the Book of Daniel. Christ is revealed again and again, and the Church embraces these passages designed to transform man into the likeness of God. Time after time in the three accounts above, Christ descends and enters the grave alongside man in order to share in his sufferings and deliver him into the light of the resurrection. The only true response man can give is to give thanks and proclaim that His mercy endures forever.

Conclusion

Our journey together is complete, but let this be the starting point of your exploration. We have taken a quick plane ride over a landscape that encompassed seven hundred years and nations stretching from Persia to Egypt. We peered in on the lives of kings and paupers, the righteous and sinners, widows and orphans. Each excursion was but a brief touchdown focused on major landmarks. Now it is time for you to reenter these stories and wise sayings at leisure, picking up a flower to examine its beauty or smelling the dust of an ancient city and feeling the desperation of those waiting for God.

As mentioned early in the discussion, the Church has used these books in preparation for baptism and entry into the life of the Body of Christ. The struggles of the Maccabees, Esther, Tobit, and many others mirror the struggles Christians face. The Church is asking those about to walk into the waters of baptism whether they are ready for the days ahead. Battle and struggle characterize this life of Christ, and death may result; but for those willing to join themselves with the God of the universe, resurrection is the outcome.

Wisdom is present here in stories and teachings, waiting to be consumed and used to create movement toward God and neighbor. These accounts prepare us for a life of virtue. They proclaim in a loud voice that life in the Church is not for the weak in heart but for the weak in Christ. Weakness and inability characterized many of the lives we have studied, but in spite of this, these men and women were willing to take a step of courage—only to have it transformed into perfect strength and victory. This is the model for us all. The life of Christ is available to all, but a step into the jaws of death is required for weak and sinful man to attain it. It is in the arena facing wild beasts, in the throne rooms of tyrants, or in the dirty streets of Persia that one finds Christ thrusting forth His hand into the light of resurrection.

Pick up and read these books again, praying for courage and transformation. Be willing to take action in the face of certain defeat, trusting in the mighty arms of our Savior.

# *Acknowledgements*

Thank yous are in order for this book. First, thank you to my parents, who instilled in me a lifelong love for the Word of God. Also, to all those pastors, teachers, coaches, youth ministers, etc., who taught me to read and teach others the Scripture.

Thank you to Fr. Alexander Atty for bringing us into Orthodoxy and giving me the opportunity to teach for many years.

Thank you to the people of St. Michael's Orthodox Church in Louisville, Kentucky, for all the encouragement during the years. The first word would never have been written without the prodding of Dr. Tad Dryden. Dianne O'Regan, thanks for reading and gently correcting; I wish I had found you sooner. Kevin Edgecomb, thank you for directing me to the proper scholarly works on this subject.

A final thanks to the adult Sunday school class at St. Michael's: Thank you for giving me the opportunity to study and teach each week. Thank you for letting me test this material on you; your insights during class were invaluable to helping me understand more deeply.

# *About the Author*

Theron Mathis is a graduate of Liberty University with a BS in Religion, and of Southern Seminary with an MDiv. He participated as a translator on the Old Testament portion of the Orthodox Study Bible as well as contributing study notes. Theron is a member of St. Michael the Archangel Orthodox Church in Louisville, Kentucky, where he has been involved in adult education for the past ten years.

Conciliar Media Ministries hopes you have enjoyed and benefited from this book. The proceeds from the sales of our books only partially cover the costs of operating our nonprofit ministry—which includes both the work of **Conciliar Press** and the work of **Ancient Faith Radio.** Your financial support makes it possible to continue this ministry both in print and online. Donations are tax-deductible and can be made at www.ancientfaith.com.

 ANCIENT FAITH RADIO

Internet Based Orthodox Radio:
Podcasts, 24 hour music and talk stations,
teaching, conference recordings, and much more,
at www.ancientfaith.com